IMPRISONMENT

SAMUEL WOODS

IMPRISONMENT
BY SAMUEL WOODS
Editing and Interior Layout: Urban Book Editor
Illustrator of Cover Image: James Jackson
Cover Designer: Tom Mcgrath

Copyright © 2020 by Books by the Shelf.
All rights reserved. No part of this book may be used or reproduced by any means, graphic, electronic, or mechanical, including photocopying, recording, taping, or by any information storage retrieval system without the written permission of the publisher except in the case of brief quotations embodied in critical articles and reviews.

Published by Books by the Shelf, Chagrin Falls, Ohio.

Printed in the United States of America.

ISBN-13: 978-1-7351097-0-1
ISBN-10: 1-7351097-0-3

Library of Congress Control Number: 2020908918

10 9 8 7 6 5 4 3 2
First Edition

I have tried to recreate events, locales and conversations from my memories of them. In order to maintain their anonymity in some instances I have changed the names of individuals and places, I may have changed some identifying characteristics and details such as physical properties, occupations and places of residence.

Dedication

This book is dedicated to everyone who may have lost a loved one to gun violence. All my people walk with me through the spirit and soul, you are never dead. You now live through me. Until we meet again, I love y'all!

RIP (Rest in Plushness)

Brian "Fat B" Limoli, Ivan "VZE The Don" Munford, Cleveland "Champayne" Hawthorne, Mike "Mikey" Cheeks, Diamond Singleton, Scott "Cope" Copely, William "Trill" Broyles, William Lee, Rick Flowers, Ed "Diggs" Charles, Eric "Eric T" Grimes, Lester "Les Red" Kolb, Nigel "Milez Boy" Jackson, Monte "Boss Man" Pitts, Kris Mayle.

Acknowledgments

I've been on one hell of a journey. A lot of people have been there for me throughout my incarceration. For that alone, I would like to thank them. Even if you are not here for me now, it doesn't matter because God placed you in my life when I needed you!

Big Thanks to my family and friends for being there for me. Marlow Freeman, Dustin Bentley, Shirlina Kelley, Lamuel Flowers, Deez, Justin & Cordero Bush, JB, Black, Cooks, Ray P., Jasmine "JD" Watkins – Thanks for rolling the red carpet out for me when I came home. Until you're free, I love you beyond death, fuz! Antoine Parker, Trumaine and Nelson White, David Gardner, Twann Smalls, Terron Duncan, Stephen Giles, Jeremy Pleasant, Jerry Pleasant, Anthony "AR Deville" Banks, Ashley Glenn, Ricardo Hunt, Clive &,Storm Sanders, Amber Walls, Jon Hearing, Jarvis Mack, Shawna Becker, Landis Coppinger, Foo Foo, Isaiah Bush, Jermaine Pleasant, Nakue Willis, my sister and brother in law, Tricia and Keith Gardner, Tom Bennett, Anthony Bennett, Big Cleveland Watkins. To my sister, Ebony Leaphart, and my brother and sister in law Tommy and Richelle Woods, I love you and everything you've been doing. I'm beyond proud, bro. Also, my forever sister in law, Michelle Woods I love and miss you and will never forget you. My niece, Quoya Woods, I thank you so much for always coming through for your uncle. Thanks for everything you have done for me. You're the realest. Thomasina Woods, thanks for never giving up on me and for making sure you came to see me even though you were living in a whole other state, thank you I love you so much! Neeka Woods, Kierra Woods, Na Leaphart, Sierra Maske, Desiree Gilham thanks for making sure things got done when needed them done. I'll never forget that. I want to thank Mondo, MG, Bird Obama, Butta, Boo Gotta, my fuz Li'l James, BG,

Farrah, Jerry "Juice" Gordon. Trey Nel, Che'la Edwards, fuz Eric, fuz Cup, fuz Skyler, fuz Chaz, fuz Nate Watkins. Free my Italian homey Chad Mayle.

I want to thank my Godmother, Lisa Bush. Big thanks to Reese for bringing the kids and mom to come to see me even though I was four hours away. Free Baby James from the Yo. My Sister Sammesha Wright, sorry we really didn't get to spend that needed time together. I promise this time we will do it bigger than ever. Forgive your li'l bro. To Matthew Dunnerstick, thanks for never judging me and accepting me for who I am and not for where I was. Love you, bro. Auntie Tiny, thanks for always having a place for me when I needed it!

I want to thank Larry for being there for me when I needed him and for loving my aunt the way that he does. Thanks to Chris "Goldie" Harris for always coming through for me when needed it.

Big Tone, PFK for life, bro!

Paper, Bone, to the big homey Alfred "Mann" Givens, one day you will be free. Love you, big bro.

I have got to thank James Jackson for drawing a vivid picture that made a powerful cover. Thanks, bro. You the truth with that pen. Thanks to my Uncle Lorenzo Snell, Thanks to my Aunt Sharon.

I want to thank my editor, Michele Barard, for the countless hours spent on this book. I know you had to work extra hard because I was all over the place, but you helped bring all my thoughts to life, and I am so appreciative of it. I am also grateful for all the knowledge you have given my wife and me throughout this project. You taught us so much and helped us with so many things when you didn't even have to. We will forever be in debt to you. I thank you dearly for everything. You truly are a blessing.

My nephews, Dontez Woods and Sinatra (Lil Joe) Leaphart, I love y'all! Shout out to my nephew, Tommy Woods, Jr. I'm proud of you. Keep working hard. You the next Stephen Curry, for REAL! My cousins, Shantia Montgomery, thanks for always going out your way for me and for always believing in me, fuz. I appreciate everything! Special thanks to my cousin Clarence "Smoody" Holcombe, thanks for everything I'll never forget all the things you did for me. I love you, fuz! To Rencie Holcombe, my aunts Angela Mallory, Cathy Currie, Cathy Cooper, and to my aunt Sharon Backie, I want to thank you for all the love and support. You were always there for me no matter what, and I want to say I appreciate it dearly from the bottom of my heart. To the rest of the

Backie family, I love all of you, and I appreciate everything. Shanell Backie, thanks for always being there for our son when I couldn't due to my incarceration. You always held it down. To Jennifer and Anthony "Pig" Lackey for being there for my daughter her whole life. It was y'all that held her down for me all these years, and I thank y'all from the bottom of my soul. I love y'all, and I'm forever grateful for the unconditional love that y'all gave my daughter and for shaping her into a wonderful woman. Thanks again, I'm forever in debt to you guys. To Stacy Miller, for giving birth to my beautiful daughter.

Special Thanks to my beautiful mother, Gloria Parker. I am so grateful to have such a strong and understanding mother like you in my life. I appreciate everything you have ever done for me, all the sacrifices you made for me and just for always supporting me and never giving up on me. I love you so much mother love!! Thanks for holding me down like no other!

Also, I would like to thank my lovely wife, Ashley Woods, for believing in me from the very first day. You never cared about how much time I was serving, but you were more concerned with what we need to do to get me home, and I love you so much for always being supportive. When it felt like we had everybody and everything going against us, you never gave up or folded! You stood by my side through everything. All the sacrifices you made, all the countless hours you worked to save money for us, from finding the attorney to making sure we had an editor for my book who understood my vision. Thank you for giving me the inspiration that I need to make it through every day and all the strength, love, and loyalty you give. You are so amazing, and I love you and will cherish you until the day I die. Thank you, baby!

To both of my grandmothers Kate Hendrix and Sarah Williams, I love both of y'all and thank you both.

To my son Sam, I want you to know that I love you very much and I am proud of the man you have grown to be. I can't wait to see you. Conquer the world!

To my beautiful daughter, Daeshona, my little rider, my mini-me, my best friend, thank you for always having your dad's back. I am so proud of the young lady you have grown to be, and I love you. Keep striving for greatness, and never stop believing in yourself!

David "Dae Dae" Varner, Cal "PDT" Lige, Neno, Trev, Bryson & Jimmy Salters (RIP miss and love both of yall every day). RIP to my father Sam Snell, my Aunt Jimmie Snell, my Uncle Warren

Currie, Darnell Currie, Henry Lee, my second mom, Irene Bentley, my uncle, Tom Snell, and Nobia Hunt.

Free all those who are wrongly convicted or railroaded in this corrupted system. Your time is coming. Never stop fighting! James B Gizzle Goins (424294) CEO of Bound by Loyalty & Womb has been down since the age of 16 for non-homicide offenses and currently serving year 20 out of 84 years. John Shakim Biowebster Edwards (674225) serving year 25 of a Life sentence, Xavier "Polo Zae" Penwell (594019) serving year ten of a life sentence, Ladarrious "Lucci" Dorsey (662000) serving year six of a 26-year sentence, Marquise "Fat Head" Perry serving year 16 of a 28-year sentence, Lee Darrington serving year 16 of a life sentence, Willy Rembert serving year 34 of a life sentence, Alfred "Man" Givens serving year 21 of a life sentence, Kevin Moore serving year 21 of a life sentence, Ryan "Pico" Watkins serving year 21 of a life sentence, Marcus "Money Mark" Ballock serving year 19 of a Life sentence, and Julius "Hook" Webster, serving 99 years.

Table of Contents

Introduction 11

Chapter 1: Less Fortunate 15

Chapter 2: Scared Straight.. 21

Chapter 3: Hard labor... 29

Chapter 4: The Transition 35

Chapter 5: Beaver Local 43

Chapter 6: Down Hill... 49

Chapter 7: Hard Time... 57

Chapter 8: Freedom Stricken.. 63

Chapter 9: Bossman 69

Chapter 10: Solitary Confinement 77

Chapter 11: Worst of the Worst 85

Chapter 12: Systematic Struggle 95

Chapter 13: Revolving Doors to a Crippled Society 101

Chapter 14: A Mind Is a Powerful Thing to Waste 111

Chapter 15: Ambitious Mind 115

Chapter 16: Purpose and Perseverance 119

Chapter 17: Life Goes On 123

Chapter 18: Fighting Demons 127

Chapter 19: Green-Eyed Blessings 131

Chapter 20: Elevate, Execute, and Expand 137

Chapter 21: Guiding Generations 141

Chapter 22: Activist Spirit 145

Introduction

Mr. Samuel Woods has written a fascinating and educational book about prison, how the prison system works, and what he has experienced while incarcerated as a repeat offender. Mr. Woods goes into detail about how the criminal justice system has affected minorities for many years. He holds nothing back and tells it like it is. His mind-blowing revelations about the way justice is served in America may force you to rethink your trust in the judicial system.

Mr. Woods offers much to think about in this book. He talks about the cycle blacks have been trapped in since the inception of chattel slavery in the United States of America, and what black people need to do to break it. He discusses how our communities have suffered and what we need to do to change the dynamic. Change is vital, not just in our lives but in this world in general. From the beginning of this book to the end, Mr. Woods takes you on a journey inside the prison world. The knowledge, honesty, and courage to write such a powerful book speaks volumes.

Nobody talks about incarceration in Ohio. The purpose of this book is to enlighten us on the horrible way the prison system runs, and how the courts are treating citizens and non-citizens alike. There is genuinely no such thing as justice in Ohio. Young black citizens have been treated as less than some of our peers. Working-class and poor neighborhoods tend to experience high crime rates, and little seems to help the numbers go down. A robust prison system fails to resolve the problems; instead, it is designed to keep us at a standstill and on our backs. The crooked system wants to make sure we never get on our feet.

Most of us are aware there are three main economic classes, the rich, the middle class, and the poor. The old saying "the rich get richer, and the poor get poorer" seems even more relevant today than in the past. The poverty and desperation of low-income housing fuels the increase in the incarceration numbers. When is this going to change? Why hasn't anyone found a solution to these conditions suffered in low-income communities? The injustice system may call us losers, but they must cheat to win. Mr. Woods explains what that statement means later in this book. Right now, let's start with why the prison rate at an all-time high.

Imprisonment

Part 1: The Less Fortunate

Samuel Woods

Imprisonment

Chapter 1: Less Fortunate

The less fortunate are those who live in low-income housing. What is low-income housing? Low-income housing is a neighborhood in which most of the people who live there are minorities and have minimum wage jobs or are unemployed. They live on Section (8) and get help from the government. I've grown up under the same circumstances many black people live under right now. Being less fortunate causes one to struggle, and that struggle can attract undesirable things into one's life.

People who grow up in poverty are caught in a vicious cycle. Single mothers are raising kids on their own and trying to provide for their families. The kids' fathers may be dead, in prison, or perhaps just walked out on them. The cycle keeps repeating itself. I'm living proof.

I grew up in a crazy hood and was exposed to drugs, prostitution, and crack houses. There were no mansions, homes, or condos on the west side of Canton, Ohio. My mother was a single mother with four kids; only two of us, my sister Ebony and me, had the same father. Our father had been murdered when we were toddlers, so we grew up without him. My older sister, Tricia, still had her father, but he was never around. Neither was my older brother Tommy's dad. We were all raised by our mother; trying to feed four kids, often on her own, was hard. I saw my mother struggle time and time again. Not only did she struggle with the fact she had to take care of us on her own, but she also struggled with drug and alcohol addiction.

Nineteen ninety-five and 1996 had to have been the two roughest years my family and I have ever suffered. In 1995, we were living in a mouse and roach-infested apartment building. It was in downtown Canton next to a bunch of other prominent buildings. I don't know how my mom found this place, but my mom, Ebony, and I were living in a one-bedroom apartment. Trish was living downstairs in a one-bedroom apartment with my two nieces and my nephew. My sister and I used to sleep in the same bed facing opposite directions, toes-to-head and head to toes. The bed was next to the kitchen, which was almost as small as the bathroom. We shared the dining room, sleeping next to the dining table. Mom was out of work, so she fed us and paid the bills using her first of the month check, which was no more than $300. Her boyfriend, at that time, was named William. He used to help, but he was abusive and had a severe crack cocaine problem. He beat my mom and hit on me on the daily. This was when my anger started to build up. My resentment and hatred toward him and the world ignited within me.

We lived in that apartment for only six to nine months, but it seemed like a lifetime. Trish had found a duplex on 4th street in Shorb Northwest. She made it out of that hell hole but didn't move into a better place. She ended up living right in the middle of gangs, drugs, and prostitution. This is where my journey began.

In 1996, we went to live with my sister Trish in a two-bedroom duplex. With my mom, Ebony, Trish, her three kids, and me in that little two-bedroom place, it was tight. I think we moved in with my sister after William checked into rehab. She had been struggling with the rent, so there we were all packed into this mouse and roach-infested duplex. I slept on the couch. I know my mom wasn't feeling this living with her daughter. I know she was stressing because she was always drinking and cussing me out. It seemed like I was getting yelled at all day every day. I took all that anger I had built up and headed to the streets, the same streets my mom was telling me to avoid. I had been running around the hood already. I was not getting into trouble, but I was hanging around kids my age who were bad as hell.

I was 12 years old going on 13 with no positive male figures around. My older brother was living on his own. My uncles all smoked cracked except for my uncle, Darnell, but he was a gangster. He could only teach me how to cook crack, sell crack, shoot guns, and drink liquor. My life took a dramatic turn for the worst.

Growing up on the west side of Canton was a challenge within itself, and here I was 12 years of age running around with no sense of direction. Shorb Block was one of the toughest hoods in Canton.

Imprisonment

It swallowed me fast, so fast I didn't even last a whole year before I caught my first case. In the first couple of months, I lived with my sister. My crew used to ride bikes we had stolen because none of our parents had money to buy us bikes. My boys and I also took pit bulls. We snatched up any puppies we came across and sold them. We stole different kinds of bikes, Dyno, Huffy, Mongoose, all the best bikes at that time. If you had one, we would take it. This was my first real taste of breaking the law and doing things I knew would get me into trouble. I had been stealing Sega games from kids I went to school, but I had stepped up my game. I was in the streets taking bikes and pit bulls and running around without a care in the world, not really understanding or even thinking about the outcome. We avoid thinking about the consequences until we get caught, but at that age, I thought I would never get caught.

One day, one of my boys from my crew rolled up on me and said, "Yo, Sam, I just seen Jesse and Jance standing out in front of the crib."

Jesse and Jance were brothers from the hood. Jance and I had some words at school a couple of days prior. I wanted to beat his ass for talking shit, so I hopped on my bike and rushed over to his house. Just like my boy said they were standing on the porch. I didn't even say anything. I just hopped off my bike, ran up on the porch, and started punching Jance. His brother ran inside the house. Finally, I threw Jance off the porch, and he rolled off the bushes to the ground. I figured that was enough, so I let him get up and run in the house behind his brother. They both stood in the window, yelling at me.

"Fuck you! You didn't do shit!" They went on just talking shit.

I noticed both of their bikes were on the side of the house. I told my boy to grab one, and I grabbed the other one. We rolled them to his house and hid them in the back behind some tall bushes. I shot back to my sister's and was chilling, acting as if nothing had happened. About an hour later, the police were knocking on my sister's door, asking for me.

My sister ran into the kitchen and said, "Sam, what the hell you do, boy?"

I gave her a confused look and said, "I ain't done nothing."

"Well, the police outside talking 'bout you done beat somebody up and took they bike." As she said this, the police walked into the house as we walked toward the front door.

"Sam Woods?" the police officer said to me as he reached for his handcuffs.

I replied, "Yea, why? What's up?"

"Well, can you put your hands behind your back for me, please? You're being placed under arrest for assault and battery and robbery."

"What? Robbery! I ain't rob or assault nobody." Although I pleaded my case, they weren't trying to hear that shit.

My mom was yelling at the cops. I could hear her saying, "Robbed who? He said he ain't robbed nobody, got damn it!"

"What the hell going on?" my other sister, Ebony, said. "What he do, y'all?"

It was crazy seeing my family as they watched me get shoved into a police car at the age of 12. The cops drove right to my boy's house. He was sitting in the back of another police car looking scared. He was only 11. I could see the cops putting the bikes in the trunk of the vehicles. I wondered how they knew where to find the bikes. They then drove me to Jessie and Jance's house, probably so they could identify me as the one who fought him and took the bikes. I could see them pointing and nodding their heads as the cop approach them. It was over. I was going to jail. At that moment, I wasn't scared. I felt a little nervous but not frightened. After Jance and Jesse identified us, the cops took us to the juvenile detention center called Fair Crest. When we arrived, I knew that it is real. It wasn't a dream or a joke. I was about to be put in jail.

Fair Crest was scary, even looking at it from the outside. I used to hear guys talking about it, and from their stories, I knew it wasn't a place I wanted to be. My heart pounded fast and hard when the cop pulled me from the back seat of the squad car. My boy had been transported in the other cop car. He was crying. Nothing like this had ever happened to him either. As I walked to the front door, it felt like everything was moving in slow motion. I was walking slowly, and the cops were talking slowly. Every window on the detention center was dark so that you couldn't see inside. Dirty, smoke-grey bricks made up the exterior of the building, which made it look like a haunted house.

After one of the cops pushed the buzzer, we heard a loud click. Then, the door opened. The cop had a tight grip on the inner part of my arm underneath my armpit. We walked through the first door and then waited for another one to open. A white guy with a long ponytail approached us. He opened the door and gave my boy and

Imprisonment

me a look like we were the scum of the earth. I knew we were in for one hell of a ride.

Samuel Woods

Imprisonment

Chapter 2: Scared Straight

The cops sat us in steel chairs, and then they left. *It's on, now,* I thought to myself. I was there, and I was not about to walk out of here. I had been keeping my hopes up the whole time, but when I saw the cops leave, I knew for sure I was staying, and nothing was going to change that. From the outside, you couldn't tell that I was scared. Although my face said *I'm ready for whatever* and *I don't care*, my heart was beating fast and I was nervous as hell.

My eyes couldn't stop wandering over every inch of the place. There were two wings of the building. The room we were in was small. It had a desk with a computer. The man who greeted us at the door sat typing something, probably our names. I saw a juvenile mopping the floors and another one wiping windows down, one was black, the other one was white. They didn't look much older than me. They were staring at us; they were trying to find out who we were. I was trying to see if I knew them as well.

"Okay, which one of y'all is Sam Woods?" the white guy said.

"That would be me,'" I responded as I looked him in the eyes.

He stared at me for little while then said, "Let me guess. This your first time coming to Fair Crest. Am I right?"

Damn! How can he tell? Wait a minute. He already knew because he seen it on the computer. I thought to myself. When I answered, my throat was dry, and my words came out a little cracked and broken up. "Ummm, yeah, ummm, yeah, this my first time. How could you tell?" I asked. I was curious. I wanted to know if I was looking scared, even though I thought I wore a serious face.

"Well, you're no more than 12-years-old, and I could see your heart busting out of your chest since you sat down. Now, listen,

I'm about to ask you some questions, okay? Then we gonna get you a cell and everything, okay? Don't ask me shit about your case because I don't know shit about your case. I'm not your lawyer. That's their job, and I don't do nobody's job but my fucking own. You got it?"

Damn, I thought. The dude was a dick, and I didn't like him just because of the way he said what he said. He then asked me all types of stupid ass questions. Did I feel suicidal or like hurting myself? Did I have any diseases? Was I allergic to anything? After he read that stupid ass shit me, he yelled to one of the other juveniles that were cleaning to get me a bedroll.

The white kid brought me two black wool blankets and one white sheet. After that, another guy who worked there came and told me to walk with him. My stomach was doing flips. I was nervous as hell as I walked through the doors then we made a left turn down the hall it was oddly quiet, and I could see the cells. We came to a door, and he told me to go inside. It was dark. I didn't know what to expect, but he then said that I had to get naked so he could search me. He made me squat and cough. Then he took all my clothes except my socks and boxers. He made me place my clothes in a metal crate and then put it on the shelf.

We walked back down the hall. I saw the other juveniles all looking out of a little plastic window on the far-right side of their cells. I walked until I reached the end. "Right here," the black guy said as he unlocked the door.

I walked into the tiny brick cell. I thought I was going to be sleeping on a metal bed, but it was bricks made into the shape of a bed and had a thin green mat on top.

"BOOM!" The sound of the door shutting hard behind me made me jump. I quickly turned around. "Now listen, Woods, don't get to yelling out this door to none of these knuckleheads, you hear? You heard how quiet it was when you walked yo ass down here, right? That's how it better stay. Don't make me come back down here. You got it?" he said sternly.

I didn't say anything; I just nodded my head up and down and then walked away from the cell door. The loneliness started to overcome me as I sat down on the mat. I held my head down, looking at the floor, trying to gather my thoughts. I was trying to figure out why and how the fuck I had gotten myself into this mess. After the staff member left, I could hear guys trying to get my attention in a low whisper.

Imprisonment

"Hey, Cell One, what's yo name?"
"What they got you for?"
"What hood you from?"

I didn't answer them. I wasn't trying to kick it. I was trying to get home; that was the only thing on my mind. After about 30 minutes, they brought my boy down and put him a few cells down from me. I could hear him still pleading that he didn't do anything to the staff member. I thought to myself, *why don't this nigga shut the fuck up?*

The staff member quickly shut that down after he closed his cell door. "Shut the fuck up now while you got the fucking chance. I don't give a fuck if you didn't do whatever. Tell that shit to the judge Monday, stupid muthafucka!"

Damn, Monday, I thought to myself. *Shit, it's only Friday. That means we have to wait all the way 'til the weekend was over with before we even go in front of a judge.*

I sat quietly on my thin mat. I still hadn't put any of the blankets or sheets over it yet. I just lay there for hours deep in thought. Then the sound of somebody loudly crying broke me from my thoughts. It sounded like my boy.

"Ughhhhhh, uggghhhhhh, I want my momma. I want my momma. I want to go home! Uhhhhhhh, uhhhhhhhh!"

"What? Man, this nigga trippin'," I said to myself as I got off my mat to get closer to the door. I could tell it was him from the way he cried out for his mom. *What the fuck?* I thought. Almost everybody within the range started screaming for my boy to shut up.

They were saying things like, "Shut yo bitch ass up, nigga! We trying to sleep, bitch!" and "Nigga, yo momma can't help you now, hoe ass nigga!" They were laughing at him, just clowning him, but when we heard keys, everybody got quiet fast.

"Y'all shut this shit up down here. What the fuck going on?" the staff member said.

I could tell this was a different one. Just from the sound of his voice, I could tell he was tall and big as fuck. Mr. Johnson wasn't anybody to play with, and I found out quickly. Well, let's say my boy did.

"Boom!" He hit the door with a hard, loud smack. "Shut yo li'l ass the fuck up! You hear me, nigga? You waking my range up down here screaming and crying all loud on my muthafucking range sounding like a bitch! Now, I'm telling you. Don't make me come back down here. You hear me? Do you hear me?" he repeated in a frustrated tone.

I still could hear my boy softly sobbing as he walked off the range. It wasn't even 30 minutes before my boy started crying loudly again, screaming that he wanted his momma and wanted to go home. It wasn't long before Mr. Johnson was back at his door.

"Nigga, didn't I tell yo punk ass to shut the fuck up with all this crying on my range? Waking my range up with this bullshit, huh?" Mr. Johnson yelled. You could hear the anger in his voice. Then, I heard him unlock and open the door. He ran into my boy's room and started beating his ass. Every punch rang in the air. Mr. Johnson hit him and slammed him on the floor, all the while telling him, "Didn't I tell you to shut the fuck up? Didn't I?"

It almost sounded like he was my boy's dad, and he was giving him an ass whipping, but Mr. Johnson was a staff member, and I couldn't believe what I was hearing. My boy was screaming like crazy now, and I could hear him crying out for help for real now and screaming he was sorry. It fucked me up. I didn't know that they could put their hands on us. That shit shook me and taught me to stay the fuck out of Mr. Johnson's way.

After he beat my boy's ass, he left the range. I could still hear my boy crying. He wasn't crying because he wanted to go home. Now, he was crying because he was in pain. I lay face-down, forehead on my arm, with thoughts all that had happened racing through my mind. Hearing my boy yell all that momma shit had me wanting and missing my mom too.

I started crying quietly. Tears just started to come down my face. I hurried to wipe my eyes as if somebody could see me. I felt like a sucker crying and vowed to myself that I would never do that again. I awoke to the sound of staff members going from cell to cell calling names followed by a letter.

"Jackson, you're a D," the little chubby white staff member said as he walked to the next cell. The cells were small, and the doors had a whole bunch of holes in them in a long triangle shape that went halfway down the cell doors. You could look through them, but it was hard to see. Everybody talked through the holes when they were allowed. I'd noticed that a lot of talking wasn't allowed. I caught on to that very quickly. There was a speaker box in the upper right corner at the very top of the wall. You could talk to the staff in case of an emergency, and they can listen in on you. I was going to figure out what all the letters meant.

"Woods, you're also a D!"

"Excuse me, sir. What does that even mean?" I asked nicely.

He looked back at his paper. "Ohhhh, that's right, you new. You just came in yesterday, correct?"

"Yea," I replied.

"So, you will be a D 'til you work yo way up. You get graded on yo behavior. So, if you want to come on out of yo cell and eat at the table with some of us, then you have to at least have C. So, it's like if you want to watch TV, then you have to have at least a B. Then, if you reach A status, well, then you would be out your cell all day, and you won't go in until 11 o'clock, but that's hard work to do that. It's a lot of rules you must follow. It's mandatory workout in here, meaning you have to work out. You don't work out, then you get a bad grade, which means you will be stuck in yo cell. And, trust me, you will get tired of being in that cell. Yo grades won't start until tomorrow, so you will be eating inside yo cell today. Got it?"

"Yea, I got it," I said. I was not feeling any of the shit he just explained.

"Damn, it seemed like you had to follow a lot of shit just to get out of yo cell."

"And, oh, you just got a bad grade," he said, breaking me from my thoughts.

"Say what?"

"You heard me. You just got a bad grade," he repeated as he walked away.

"For what, man? I ain't even done nothing," I yelled out of my cell door with a little anger.

He just kept walking, not even letting me know what I had done. After that, I didn't like him at all.

Then I heard somebody whispering to me. "Aye, aye, Woods. Aye!"

"What's up? Who dat?" I responded.

"Aye, I'm right across from you. Is yo bed made up?"

I looked back and saw that my bed wasn't made. My sheet wasn't even on my bed. "No, my shit ain't made."

"Well, that's why yo ass just got that bad grade."

"How the fuck was I pose to know that, huh?"

"You wasn't. That's how they do all first-timers, man. You have to learn everything for yourself in here, man. Listen, you have to make yo bed up like they do in the army. You have to have that shit with no wrinkles and all that shit and have yo other blanket folded up eight inches or some shit at the top of yo bed, man. They serious about shit like that. Oh, shit, here comes the trays. Gotta go."

"Aye, aye, what's yo name, man?" I tried to catch his name, but I guess it was too late.

I stood up off my mat when I heard my cell door unlock. I was hungry as hell. It felt like I hadn't eaten in days. It was a cocky black kid passing the trays out. He looked very familiar as I stared at him. He stared at me as well, trying to see if he knew who I was. To my surprise, he did.

"Li'l Sam, what's up, Li'l Nigga?" The words threw me off like a muthafucka because I still couldn't recognize him. "Nigga, this Chancellor," he said as if he couldn't believe I hadn't recognized him.

"Oh, shit, what's up, man? Damn, nigga, you done got big as fuck. That's why it took me a minute," I replied with a smile. I was relieved that I finally did remember who he was. We used to live in Highland Park back in the day when I was young. Highland Park is the project in Canton, Ohio, and I did remember him. I remembered his case too.

That nigga Chancellor was crazy as hell. He was only 16 years old, but he looked like a grown-ass man. He had gotten into a high-speed chase and ran over a cop dog and killed it. I think they gave him like 25 years or some shit. They bonded him over, meaning he was going to be going to prison at 16 years old. I couldn't even imagine that shit. Even though he had all that time, he seemed calm. He was smiling and everything. My situation wasn't anything close to his, and I was crying like a little bitch. Seeing him made me man up.

"Here, Li'l Sam, I'm a come back to talk to you when we clean up the cells, alright."

"Yea, alright, "I said, looking at the little ass tray of food he had given me. "Man, what the fuck is this shit?" I said.

The tray was metal but thin. It had five slots for the food, a square for the bread, a rectangle next to that where the main course would go or like for breakfast oatmeal or cereal, and three small slots above the bread and main course slots. All the slots were tiny. Chancellor also gave me one cup of orange juice and one cup of milk. The containers were so small you wouldn't even be able even to taste the shit.

I sat on my mat and stared at the tray. The only thing that was good about it was the bread was toasted. The one scoop of oatmeal

Imprisonment

was dry and wasn't going to fill a 5-year-old's stomach. I was pissed, but I smashed the food and then drank the milk. I tried to follow it up with the orange juice, but I quickly spit that shit onto the tray. The orange juice was nasty as hell. It was sour. I had never tasted orange juice like that before, and I vowed to myself that I wouldn't ever drink that shit again.

After about 20 minutes, they started to pick up the trays. Then, they started cell clean-up. They give you a bottle of cleaning chemicals and a broom with a dustpan. My cell wasn't dirty as I would have thought it would have been, but I made sure I cleaned the toilet and the mat well.

While I was cleaning, Chancellor told me what had happened to him. I felt sorry for him. He was only 16 and about to go to prison and for a long time. He was telling me how things were run. He told me just to follow the rules and stay out of trouble and how he couldn't believe I was locked up. He said they ran this shit like the military, really strict.

"What? Nigga, they don't run this like no muthafucking military," I cut in when he said that.

"Shit, how you think I got this size? I've been here going on a year, nigga. They 'bout to work yo li'l boney ass," he spat with a slight laugh.

"Listen, my li'l nigga, just pay attention and fuck trying to kick it with these dudes. They all weak. You hear me? Just chill and do what you gotta do to get out of here."

I shook my head as I handed him the broom and bottle.

"So, what they got you on?" he asked.

"Man, I beat this white boy up and took his bike an' shit. He called the police on me. I can't believe he did that shit."

"Well, believe that shit, my li'l nigga. Shit, they always gonna tell, man. I heard yo boy was crying all night. What the fuck is up with that?" he said, clowning him.

"Man, I don't even know. That nigga was tripping for real."

"Yea, he was heard. Mr. Johnson fucked his ass up." Chancellor started laughing. "Listen, stay out of his way. He don't like nobody, alright. And when you get out, because y'all both 'bout to get out, leave that sucka alone. That nigga weak. I wouldn't be surprised if that nigga told something, too."

It didn't hit me until Chancellor said that. I started thinking about how they knew where the bikes were and where my sister's house was because neither Jessie nor Jance knew. *Damnnn! This nigga told everything, stupid ass nigga!* I thought to myself. I couldn't believe it, but after hearing him cry all night like that, it didn't come as much as a surprise. The nigga snitched on me. That would happen a lot in my lifetime dealing with the streets.

"Aye, listen, Li'l Sam, I gotta go, so peep. You will go to court Monday. Plead not guilty and just chill. Wait it out. You will be cool. They not going to come to court on you. Trust me. You probably gonna be here for, like, a month though, but it beats getting time and getting sent to The Hills or The River." Those were prisons for juveniles. He continued, "Look, I gotta go, man. Talk to you later. Don't forget what I said."

"I gotcha. I gotcha," I replied.

I felt a lot better after talking to Chancellor. Although he helped clear my mind on a lot of things, it still didn't prepare me for the next few weeks I had to spend in this hell hole.

Imprisonment

Chapter 3: Hard labor

Boom! Boom! "Get Up! Get the Fuck Up!" was all I heard. Keys banged against the cell doors. It was loud as fuck and woke me up from my sleep. I quickly jumped to my feet to see what the hell was going on. I couldn't see through the tiny window, but I could see the light from outside. It was pitch black outside, so I knew it was still early as fuck. It couldn't have been more than 5 a.m.

"You guys got five minutes to have your beds made up nice and tight. I don't want to see a fucking wrinkle in that shit. Then, we going to fall in line to the front room. Workout time, gentlemen, staff member Mr. Johnson yelled with a laugh.

I hated that nigga. He thought he was the shit, but I thought he was a bitch, too, just like my mom's boyfriend, William. He was light-skinned, tall, and mean, just like William. It felt like I was at home because of all this abuse we endured. I quickly made my bed up so I could be ready. I had my bed tight real tight. I double-checked to make sure I made no wrinkles in my blanket and that my other blanket was eight inches right in the middle of the top of my mat. Everything was perfect.

"Now, listen, you li'l muthafuckas. I'm only saying this shit once. You hear me? We going four cells at a time. You each will be given two minutes to piss, brush yo teeth, all that shit. Then, when I say time, you better be lined the fuck up single file ready to get the fuck out of my bathroom. You got it? Now, let you not be in line. That ass gonna be stuck in that muthafuckin' cell."

As I was listening to Mr. Johnson scream all this shit to us, I was wondering when I was going to get my clothes. I was still in my T-shirt, boxers, and socks. The sound of cells being opened echoed throughout the whole range. I was in cell one, so I thought my door would have been the first one to be opened, but he started from the back. I was happy because it gave me a chance to watch what the hell we had to do. If anybody made a mistake, I would know what not to do.

The first few dudes came out single-file. They were standing straight and facing forward without speaking. You could hear a pin drop it was so quiet. Then he permitted them to walk toward the bathroom. There were eight of them; four juvies on each side of the hall. I watched them walk past my cell. They looked a little afraid and very focused. It was intense, and just like he commanded, they were allotted two minutes, nothing more or nothing less. They were back in their cells in a matter of minutes. I thought, *Damn, these muthafuckas ain't playing.* They keyed the next couple of cells, and I saw my boy walk past. He had the saddest look on his face. He looked depressed like he was ready to hang himself after just a couple of days in lockup. It was a sad sight to see my boy looking so weak, but I didn't have time to worry about him. I had to make sure I was on point. Then, just like I thought, he didn't follow instructions, so they threw his ass back in his cell before he could even brush his teeth or anything. I just shook my head in disappointment.

I was coming up next, and I was ready to handle mines. Soon, my door got keyed. I stepped out of my cell and faced the bathroom. I kept my hands at my sides and my chin up. I must say I even impressed myself with how I picked everything up and was on point with everything. As I looked ahead, I saw the other staff member sitting in front of the bathroom with a box in his hand. He put a little bit of toothpaste on the end of the toothbrushes and handed them to us as we walked into the bathroom.

I was mad as hell about that little ass shit he had given me. It wasn't even enough to get my mouth wet. What made it worse was that he didn't even hand us a washrag. I didn't hear anybody else ask about it, so I just went into the bathroom. I quickly took a piss. It felt like I had been holding that piss for a week. I then hurriedly washed my hands and brushed my teeth. "Talking about hard labor," I said to myself. As I hurried back into my line, I saw Chancellor. He was leading the line.

After we finished brushing our teeth, we sat in our cells for about 15 minutes. Then Mr. Johnson came back down the range with all that unnecessary yelling. He used to try to scare everybody with all that loud-ass yelling. I'm not saying he didn't scare me, but he was a bully as far as I was concerned. He prayed on young kids who didn't know how to defend themselves, especially against a big, grown-ass man.

"Alright, muthafuckas, listen the fuck up! We 'bout to go do our mandatory workout, which means everybody get yo ass up. If you don't want to work out, then you already know yo ass stays in yo muthafucking cell. I don't give a fuck. I want you in there anyway so I ain't gotta deal with yo stupid ass. Now, line it the fuck up! Y'all know the muthafuckin' drill."

"Damn, that's all this nigga know how to say is muthafucka this muthafuckin' that," I said to myself as I stepped out of my cell into the line. We walked into the big area where I saw them cleaning when I first arrived. He had us form four lines with four or five of us in each line. Chancellor and the two I saw cleaning when I got here on my first day stood in front.

Chancellor began, "Alright, this is the mandatory workout. For those of y'all that has been out here, y'all know how we do it. We get to it. We don't start a new routine until everybody finishes the one before, so you better keep up. That goes for you, Li'l Sam.

What? What the fuck he say my name for all loud and shit? That nigga tripping, I thought as I gave him "a nigga you trippin'" look. He commanded us to do this crazy workout routine of 50 push ups and 100 mountain climbers. Man, I fell out after the first 20 push ups. I hadn't worked out since I played little league football and basketball the year before. I was weak, and it showed. I tried, but I couldn't keep up. Everybody had to wait for me to finish my sets, and it took forever for me to finish. Even the skinny white boys were doing more than me. I felt like a sucker struggling the way I was, but I didn't quit, although that's all Chancellor and the other two workout instructors kept yelling.

"Quit, Sam, quit! Li'l nigga, you holding everybody up! Nigga, just quit."

"Yea, man!" the rest of the juvies yelled as my face fell to the ground after I finished the last set of push ups. I got off the ground with my face covered in sweat. My body was sore and hurting, yet I hadn't quit.

"Alright, everybody know we finish strong with 150 jumping jacks. Let's go!" Chancellor said as everybody started doing their jumping jacks at the same time. I was so tired. I knew I wasn't going to be able to keep going. After I reached around 60, I stopped and bent over to catch my breath. It felt like I was about to throw up that little bit of breakfast I had eaten, but I started jumping again. Then, it happened. I threw up all over the floor.

They let me have it! These dudes clowned me like crazy. I had to redeem myself and fast. It made me look weak, and I didn't want anybody ever to think I was weak. After that day, I vowed never to throw up again. I started doing a workout in the cell to build my strength up, so I could be ready for whatever workout they threw at us.

After our workout, we took showers. I swear I never hated washing my ass until the day I had to stand in line naked waiting for two minutes for the next set of threes to get into the shower. Standing behind one naked guy with another naked guy standing behind me made me feel violated. I felt crazy as hell standing there. I think being in such a vulnerable position made me resent being locked up. I was so mad at myself for putting myself in this situation. It created a lot of hatred inside of me. I used that anger to make it through the next few weeks.

On Monday, my mother showed up on my court date. It wasn't like anything happened. I walked into a room with a lawyer and prosecutor. Seeing my mother sitting there made me emotional. I knew she was mad at me because she didn't even smile at me when I first saw her. She sat behind the lawyer and me. We were at a long table with all types of folders and papers stacked on top. The prosecutor sat on the other side of us and had a lot of folders and documents stacked up on her table as well.

"Hey, Mr. Woods, my name is Jessica Taylor. I will be representing you today, okay?" I just nodded my head. "So, you know you're being charged with assault and robbery?" Again, I nodded my head. "What we will be doing today is just pleading not guilty, okay? The prosecutor is going to try to throw a deal out there, but we aren't taking any, right?" she said, giving me that "fuck no" look. I shook my head, no.

"Good, now, listen. The judge will be asking you how do you plead, and you're to say not guilty, okay?"

"Okay," I responded.

When the judge asked me how I plead, I said not guilty like she told me. The judge set my court date for two weeks after that. I would have to go to trial, and from there, see where this case was going to go. After going back and forth to court a few times, the charges were dropped because Jance never showed up. They released my boy and me, but while going back and forth to court and talking with my lawyer, I found out that my boy had told on me. I had suspected it since they knew where to find the bikes, but seeing his written statement made me mad as fuck. I wanted to kick his ass, but I just let it go. I didn't fuck with him anymore. He was no longer a part of my crew.

Samuel Woods

Chapter 4: The Transition

After being released from Fair Crest, I turned 13. Most kids my age were figuring out which school sports they would play, not me, though. I was getting introduced to crack cocaine and how to sell it. I was already smoking weed, drinking, and breaking all the rules doing things a 13-year-old had no business doing.

We were still living with my older sister. With all of us crammed into the small duplex, it felt like the place was getting smaller and smaller the longer we stayed there. My mother was in a tight spot after William left, and I felt like it was on me to help in every way possible, so I took to the streets. I already knew what I was going to do when I came home, and that was get up with the Shorb boys. I already knew the niggas who ran Shorb, so it was nothing for me to be a part of the clique. These are the options that are left today. Our communities don't leave us with many choices and have too much to offer us when you come from a broken home. We turn to the streets. It's beyond typical; it's almost a tradition.

I started hanging with some of my boys I had known years before I got out of juvie. Before I got locked up, they were talking about getting put down with the Shorb boys, so it wasn't a surprise to me when I met up with them in the hood, and they told me that they finally became a part of the block. I already had my mind made up that I was going to make that transition as well.

"What's up, Li'l Sam? What's the deal?" one of the older homies from the block said to me as I walked into the garage on 8th Street. I had known him for a long time. He wasn't the one who started Shorb, but he was one of the original members.

"You tell me! I'm trying to be a part of this Shorb shit. What's up?" I said with a lot of confidence.

"Is that right?" one of the leaders cut in. I knew him before he and his brother joined any gang or block. We all used to live near Gibbs Elementary School and Bell Stone School a few years back. That's how I knew almost all the original members of Shorb, which was initially called 5th RIP. They originated from 18th Street on the other side of town. Then they moved to 8th Street of Shorb, right in the middle of the block in the heart of the hood. I was living in the Northwest before all of this occurred, back when the Lynch Mobb Crew ran the hood. They all caught life sentences before Shorb grew and became prominent in the city. It was the new generation, and I was about to be a part of it.

"Yea, that's right. What I gotta do?" I spat with a severe face and my head high.

"Well, first off, li'l nigga, how old is yo li'l ass now, Sam?" the other brother said with a chuckle.

"Nigga, I'm 13."

"Nigga, you ain't 13 yet," he said, and everybody started laughing.

"Nigga, I'm 13 like I said, man. Fuck all that. What's up? Is y'all putting me down or what? Y'all niggas already put my squad down. I know my niggas already told you to make it happen."

"Yea, them niggas told me, but, nigga, if Ebony found out, nigga, she a kill us," the brother said.

"Yea! Oh, yea, I forgot about that shit, nigga. You is Ebony's li'l brother."

"Nigga trying to have his crazy ass momma come around this bitch tripping," the older homie cut in trying to play me like I was a little kid or something. In reality, I was, but it was time for me to step my shit up, and I wasn't taking no for an answer.

The next thing I knew, one of my boys from my crew punched me hard as fuck in my stomach. He caught me off guard, so I stumbled back a little. All you heard was "ouuuuuuuuuu" real loud coming from all the homies that were in the garage. There were at least 15 of us.

I quickly regained my composure and squared up with my boy. I was a little taller than him, but he had more weight on him than I did, so he was a little stronger too.

I threw some punches back, catching him in his chest. The homies were yelling "ouuuuuuuu" again. I heard one of our boys say, "Get 'em, Tec," and then he rushed me. He picked me up and slammed me hard on the ground. I was mad as fuck. That shit hurt like hell. I quickly jumped to my feet and rushed him, but instead of grabbing him, I was throwing punches. I threw so many punches he couldn't block all of them, and some of them hit him in his face. I could see he was mad. He took his shirt off and started throwing punches back, catching me in my face a couple of times. Then, one of the brothers stopped it.

"Alright! Alright!" said the brother with the light brown eyes. I thought they were his natural eye color, but I later found out he was wearing contacts. "That's enough. Okay, Li'l Sam, I see you got heart. You got a lot of heart. You think you ready, huh?" he asked.

I said, "Hell, yea, I'm ready." I was still trying to catch my breath.

"Alright, alright, this is what we gonna do."

"We gon' put you down, but you still got a lot to learn. Feel me? You need to know that this ain't no joke. You hear me, li'l nigga? This shit is real. Imma put you on today." He got to yelling niggas names and told them to take me out back and put me down. I had to follow a lot of rules and shit. I had to kneel on my left knee and get jumped by five members. They kicked my ass. I still tried to fight back, but the five of them were too much for me. They fucked me up! My head and back were hurting from getting slammed so many times, but I took it like a G. I didn't stop or give up. I kept fighting until I couldn't anymore. When I officially became a member of the Shorb Boys, I felt like I couldn't be touched by anybody or anything. This was when I started to get introduced to a lot of the things my mom used to tell me to avoid.

The brother with the light brown eyes handed me a black flag and told me to put it into the left side of my back pocket. "That's our side," he told me. "We do everything from the left." The flag separated us from our enemies, who were on the East side of the city. The enemy was from Second Street, and they were deep, really deep.

The rest of that summer, I made a name for myself for fighting. My homeboy, Tec, and I were always fighting. Tec was around my age. Out of all the homies in our crew, we grew to be the closest. We regularly got into it. We always fought each other in real fistfights. Sometimes I would kick his ass, and other times he would kick my ass, but we grew to be close, like real brothers. We were always together.

One day when I was looking for my other shoe, I came across something that I had been trying to get for some time. I had gone to my sister's room, and I was looking under her bed and came across a silver gun. I quickly put it in my pocket and left. I knew it belonged to my sister's boyfriend, Keith. I never liked him. Keith thought he was the shit, coming and going as he pleased. He thought he was that nigga or something. I didn't like any of my sister's boyfriends. Keith just was another bum trying to freeload off my sister. He thought he was cool, but his cologne stunk, and his lips were always ashy like he rubbed baby powder on them. He was a sucker. I was happy about taking his gun and didn't think twice about it. I couldn't wait to show my crew what I had found. Having that gun at my age made me feel like I owned the world. I felt like nobody could touch me. I had been infatuated with pistols for as long as I could remember, and I couldn't have been happier to own one.

Later that night, my sister and Keith rushed me with questions. "Did you see a gun in my room? Did you take a gun out my room? Were you in my room today?"

Then, this nigga Keith said, "Aye, look, Li'l Sam, if you got it, man, just give it back to me. I know you got it, Sam. Just give it back. You ain't gonna get in trouble."

I gave that nigga a look of disgust and said, "Look! I ain't got no gun, nor did I see a gun!" Then, I walked away. I rode my bike to my boy Heartless' house and stayed the night. That's where we kept all our guns.

The school year had just started, and we were all attending Lehman Middle School. I was in the 6th. Tec and Heartless were in the 7th and a year older than me. I think we all got held back once or twice, but now we were attending classes and trying to learn; at least I was. That's where Heartless, Tec, and I used to hang. It was us three for real. We were like three in one. If you didn't see Tec and me, you would see Tec and Heartless. Or you would see Heartless and me if you didn't see all of us together. We were the tightest out of our crew, which was the youngest of the whole clique. We were up and coming, and we were about to turn everything around within one year.

My mother finally found us a little three-bedroom house on the West side of Canton. Ebony and I were happy as hell to have our own rooms finally. Things were going well for a minute, but then I got deeper into the streets and the gang activity. I was barely ever home. I was 13 going on 20, and literally, had a pistol and dope sack. Dealing drugs wasn't hard at all. My hood was full of crack houses and crack users. We lived in one of the most drug-infested hoods in the city. Not only did we have crack houses, but we had a hoe strip. Prostitution was a big part of my hood. They were turning tricks up and down 6th Street all day. There were even drag queens; they call them transgender today, guys who dressed up as women and turned tricks.

Sixth Street looked like a strip in Vegas. It was jumping from morning until night. That is what my mom wanted me to stay away from, but it was too late. I had already transitioned myself over to the underworld, and once you make that transition, it's hard to go back. The streets swallow you up whole and spit you out. Let me give you an example of what I mean by that.

At 13 years of age, I was posted on the block with my boys selling crack to fiends. We were making our own money, just getting $50 double-ups. Back then, a double-up was getting five crack rocks for $50.00, so you turn that $50.00 into $100.00. That's what I started with, 50 bucks. I started making a little money, nothing major. I still was learning the game of it all. It was crazy because my mom was smoking crack. Heartless' mom smoked crack, and Tec's dad smoked crack. We all grew up together, and our parents all knew each other. They were tight just like we were. We were brothers, family, and we all went through the struggle together. It was real for us. At our young ages, we witnessed and went through things kids shouldn't have to.

That year, we built up our reputations and started getting a name for ourselves. When Heartless's mom moved into the ally off Queen is when shit started to get real for us. We were in the game deep. We were pushing crack heavily now. We had been in shoot outs with rival gangs, and we were having sex with all the cute girls in the hood. We had come up for real. I felt like I couldn't be touched. The respect I received when I went to school or just walked the streets was the best feeling I had ever felt in my life. I think that was why I stayed running the streets and I stayed in a gang. That's where I felt loved.

I put my mom through hell throughout the years I was running the streets gang banging. By the time I turned 15, I was locked up, and this time it looked like I was about to spend some time in juvie. I had been charged with assaulting the same boy who told on me in that situation when I went to Fair Crest the first time. A few guys from my crew and I finally caught up with him, and we beat him good. While we were hitting him, someone called the police. We all got arrested and charged with assault. Some of us went to juvenile prison, and some of us went to a group home. I was one of the two that went to Fair Crest. I knew I had enemies. We all did, and we had a bunch of them.

The very first night I got booked into Fair Crest, I saw one of my enemies, and the first thing that came out of his mouth was, "Damn, them the niggas that shot me right there!"

I looked at my niggas with the kind of look that said, *did you hear what this nigga said*? It was crazy. I knew there was about to be some shit. After they booked us in, they split some of us up. They had me back on the left-wing where I was the last time I was there. It was a lot different. I looked at everything differently, and some of the staff remembered me. Dave was one of the staff members. He was a short chubby white guy, and one of his best friends used to live right in the hood, so he would see us all the time. He knew us well. They had another cool staff member named Mr. Sharp. He used to play professional football, but the Browns cut him. He was 6' 5" and 230 lbs. He was big as fuck. He was cool; he just wanted us to do better. Then there was Ron. He ran the whole spot. I didn't know all this the first time, nor was I around long enough to figure any of that shit out. But there I was back again inside of a cell. I was mad as hell, pacing back and forth while thinking about what was going to happen to me. My mother was angry, and she was tired of me getting into shit.

This time I wouldn't be home for almost nine months. I spent three of those months in Faircrest while I was going through a trial for my charges. All my homies and I were on trial, and we all were found guilty. It was crazy. My old "friend" who had snitched took the stand and told the judge we beat and stomped him. I couldn't believe this nigga would do such a thing, but it was all good. I learned a valuable lesson, and that was never to trust anybody. Friends can and will turn into your enemies, so be careful who you call your boy.

Like I said, we were deep, and the niggas we were beefing with were deep as well. We had been arguing and saying shit to each other during the first couple of days. Then, we got a chance to catch up with them. My boy Doc had made a shank, which he showed me one day while we were about to start a mandatory workout.

"Brah, soon as one of these niggas try something or say anything,

I'm getting it poppin' in this bitch!" he whispered to me.

I shook my head, *hell yea!* I felt everything he said. There was so much tension in the room you could feel it. Everybody was watching one another to see who was going to make the first move, but nothing happened. The next morning when we sat down to eat breakfast, one of them sat down in front of me at the table. Doc was sitting right next to me. A couple of guys from 2nd Street sat in front of us as well. Then the one I had been arguing with spoke.

"Nigga, who shot me?" he asked angrily. Hearing this nigga ask me this shit like he was somebody I was supposed to be scared of pissed me off. I grabbed the fork off the table, and at the same time, we all stood up, Doc and me on our side, and he and his boy on the other side.

"Bitch ass nigga!!! Who shot my cousin?" I replied with fire in my eyes, looking like I was ready to kill the world.

"Aye, Aye, Ayeeeee! Y'all better step the fuck back!" Mr. Dave rushed over to us, yelling. I backed up and just looked at that nigga. After that, they kept us in the cell by ourselves. Then they started sending us to different juvenile places. I was sent to a couple of places that were way better than Fair Crest that also housed girls. I didn't want to leave, but they moved me back as soon as they could because it was time for me to get sentenced. When I got back to Fair Crest, I built my grades up, and I pretty much did whatever I wanted.

I ran the workout. I stayed out of my cell all day, and I used to draw for Ron. He used to have all the gang members from different parts of the city draw pictures for him. He was infatuated with gangs and crime, but he also was trying to give us kids a different direction to go. By that time, it was too late for us. We all had our minds made up. It was too late for us to change and take the straight and narrow route. We all were willing to die for our block. At the time, it seemed like nothing take us from that. So even though Dave, Ron, and Mr. Sharp tried their best to change our minds about being in gangs and running the streets, we didn't feel like we were ever going to change. Our moms needed help paying rent due to the fact most of them were smoking crack and had no jobs. We felt forced to sell drugs and do whatever we had to do to make money and make it through life the best way we knew how. With no positive role models, there was nobody there to teach us the righteous way to live. All of my uncles were either dealing drugs, pimping, or smoking crack. They all stayed in and out of prison ever since I could remember. All they ever taught me was how to be gangsters like them. They never showed me anything positive. What else would someone expect from me growing up in that environment with not one positive influence?

My mother knew I was going to be a handful, from getting whooped with extension cords by William, to being in gang fights and shootouts. My heart was cold, and my mind was poisoned with pain and full of anger before I even turned eighteen. Kids coming from broken communities are full of rage. They are searching for acceptance from others because they never experienced love in their households. Their moms were too busy trying to get high to pay attention to them. Their fathers were away doing time, or they just never knew him. This is the typical life for many kids coming up the way I did. Then people wonder why things like this haven't changed. Things don't change because the government runs this world, and everything is about money to them. I'll get more into all of this later in this book. Let me finish telling you how I ended up where I'm at right now and why I got here.

When I left Fair Crest, I wasn't allowed to go straight home. I was being shipped to a group home. It was full of white boys. Only two other blacks and I were in this group home, and one of them was my boy. The other black kid acted white; he was a softy. I knew he didn't come up like me and my boy did. I used to think he was gay because he had feminine ways. I didn't talk to him. I only spoke to my boy. We were close, and we both had the same amount of time to do in the home. He hated being there. Just like me, he did what he had to do to get out of there. That meant playing by their rules. I can't lie; I was able to learn things being in the group home that I probably never would have if I was back home. Going to Lehman and being around all those white people made me pay attention. I knew if I didn't do right, they would make me stay in the group home longer, so I was on my best behavior. I had to reach certain levels to get out of there, so I planned to stay out of trouble.

Chapter 5: Beaver Local

I attended a school called Beaver Local; it was an all-white school, except for me, my boy, and the other kid I mentioned earlier. That school year was crazy for me. I had to endure a lot of racial hatred being at this middle school, and I knew it wasn't going to be long before I had to defend myself. I used to like going to Beaver Local; the teachers there treated me with respect. It was like they all wanted me to do well. They paid extra attention to me. I learned a lot. I learned that I enjoyed history while I attended this school, but I still hated math. I wanted to play sports, especially basketball, but I had just missed the tryout session. It was around December when I arrived, so we were waiting for track season to start. I had never run track, but I was willing to try it out. My first few months there went smoothly. I was getting my level up and getting closer to being released. I was doing so well that I was able to get a job. My first job ever was working at a car wash. I think I made like $15 every three days. It wasn't much, but it was mine, and I was saving that money. I also got tips.

I liked working at the car wash, but I missed a lot of fun things the group was doing, like going to baseball games. I was so pissed one day when I came back to the home, and it was empty. I wondered where everybody was, and the staff there said they had gone to a baseball game. That hurt, but I didn't allow my emotions to show. I felt like they should have included me, but ever since the day I arrived, the boys there hated on me. I was different, and I was smart. I could out-think all those weak ass white boys on any given day. They were jealous of the way I was taking care of myself. One boy named Bo thought he was the shit. He was a spoiled ass white boy from a good family. He was there because he liked to steal. He wouldn't listen to his mom or dad, so they sent him to the group home. He had a smart mouth on him, and we stayed bumping heads, but I never had to beat his ass. He didn't want that he wasn't that stupid.

After the baseball game, another trip came up. We went to the museum in Pittsburgh. That was fun. We kicked it, and I learned something different. In my hood, there weren't any trips to museums. Our school field trips weren't taking us to anyplace like that, especially not to another state. I enjoyed that trip. I then started running track, and this when I started messing with different girls. Every other week I had a new girl. I can't lie. Beaver Local had some pretty white girls that attended, and they all wanted to be with me. There was one problem with that. At the group home, they had rules against having girlfriends and engaging in sex. You couldn't even kiss a girl. You couldn't cuss or disrespect anyone. And they had a group in which you had to confess if you broke any of these rules. I'm telling you this group home was crazy, but it would help someone who was trying to change their ways. In my five months of being there, I saw three different white boys run away because they hated it. I didn't understand that because after you reach your third level, you could get home visits every weekend. My boy and I started going on home visits after being there for three months. A lot of the boys came back, although we had every opportunity to run; the smart guys knew that they would be free in a matter of months. Running away never crossed my mind.

As I started breaking records in the high jump, the white boys at my school wanted to be cool with me, but a lot of them still called me a nigger, just never in my face only when they drove by me or drove by my bus when I was on it. Then one day my boy and I were on the bus. These two sisters who used to flirt with us were on the bus too. None of us ever tried to come at them, though. The older sister decided to sit in my seat, and I told her to get out of my place. I didn't want her sitting next to me. She got mad and tried to swing on me as she got up to leave. I dodged that shit, but out of nowhere, one of the white boys from the group home pushed her down the aisle. Her sister tried to slap him, and then everybody on the bus was screaming and pushing and throwing slaps in the air. That day was crazy. We didn't get into trouble dealing with that situation, but the next day, I had a funny feeling. Something wasn't going to be right. I was walking over to Beaver Local High School, which was located right across the street from the middle school. I saw four tall white boys standing outside the school, and I knew they were waiting for me.

I had my mind made up that if they came at me that I wasn't even going to talk. I would just start swinging. Before I knew it, they were walking up on me. I balled my fist up, ready for whatever. I saw that the bigger one of the four looked down at my hands, so he knew I was ready.

"What's up, nigger? So, you like hitting on girls?" he spat with anger and deceit in his voice.

I didn't hesitate. I just threw the punches at his face, connecting each one. He stumbled back. I struck him with force, so I knew he had second thoughts of trying to fight me, but he had his boys with him, so he didn't want to look like a bitch. Now that I had seen the fear in not just him but his boys too, I started talking a little shit.

"What's up, white bitches? What's up?" I ran up and started punching on him more. He tried to rush me, but I sidestepped him and hit him again this time, dropping him to the ground. After he fell, I ran up on one of the other boys that were with him. He jumped back. They couldn't believe what I just had done to their boy. After they helped him up, all the teachers ran out and stepped in front of us. They dragged me to the school and gave me a three-day suspension. Later, I found out those guys didn't even attend the school.

Back at the group home, I had to tell the group I was fighting, and they dropped my level from a four back down to a three. I didn't understand that at all, but I ended up getting back to a four in no time.

My boy and I went home in May. It felt good to be back home with my family. I was turning 16 the following month, so it was cool. I headed right back to the hood. That's all I thought about when I was there. I couldn't wait to get back to the streets. I didn't learn anything about staying out of trouble. Instead, I learned how to be more of a criminal than anything. So, at 16, I got the hood on my back. My squad was in an all-out war with the niggas from the other side. We had shoot outs; we had brawls. We were getting it in every day, shoot on sight, and I refused to get caught without my strap. We were at war the entire summer, then the fall and winter came, so the beef slowed down. The homies and I were grinding. My right hand was locked up on drug charges, so it was Heartless and me out there.

I had the hood jumping. I was flooding the dope houses around the hood and doing well for a 16-year-old. I was running through ounces like it wasn't anything. I had a spot on 6th and a spot on 4th right across the street from where my sister used to live. I had another place on 5th, and I had my stepdad, William, moving for me as well. I was selling at least two to three ounces a day.

I bought a 1983 Cutlass Supreme. It was silver with cream interior and drove like it had a 350 rocket in it. You couldn't tell me anything. I felt like I was on top of the world. I had everything. I bought my mom a brand-new living room set and an entertainment center, a microwave, and a stereo. I bought her everything with that drug money, and I helped with the rent. I had all the females. Life was great until one December night.

I was at my stepdad's apartment. William had three or four hoes working for him, so he always had money. I used to sell dope to him. That night, I wanted to spend the night with this chick I was fucking with named Kenyatta. She and her cousin, Tanna, came to my stepdad's to pick my nigga Suave and me up. I left William about $400 worth of crack so he could sell it for me. I was going to be in for the night. We left and drove to the hood.

I had left about $400 worth of dope with Diane, my other runner who sold for me. As I pulled up to the front of the house, I saw cop cars just driving slowly up 6th. I was going to walk up the stairs to see if she had my money so I could take it in and give her some more dope. I figured she was done with the dope that I had given her earlier that day. I felt something wasn't right, so I told Tanna to keep driving. As she did so, a cop car came from out of nowhere and jumped behind us. We made a right on 6th, turning onto Fulton. They followed, so I told her when she reached 8th Street to turn so I could throw the bottle of dope I had in my inside pocket out of the window. Instead, her stupid ass drove down 8th, which made it impossible to throw the drugs out the window without the cops seeing. As soon as she made that turn, they hit the lights on us.

"Damnnn," I said out loud. I was trying to work my scanner, but I couldn't find the station they were on, so I just said fuck it. "Man, I told yo ass to turn up 8th. Fuck is you doing, man?" I yelled at Tanna as I was reaching in my inside pocket to retrieve the dope, but as soon as I got to it, the cops had a big ass gun pointed at the side of my face.

"Don't you fucking move! Don't you move a muthafuckin' muscle!" the cop yelled as he opened the car door. He grabbed me so fast I couldn't even get my arm out of the inside pocket. He pinned me up against the car, open my jacket up, and pulled the bottle out. Before I could say anything, the handcuffs clamped shut, and three more cop cars arrived.

I could hear Tanna screaming and crying. She yelled, "Sam, why you have that shit in my car? I can't believe you, Sam. Why?" Tanna was boohooing. The shit had me salty as fuck. *What is she thinking? She the reason why we in this mess in the first place*, I thought.

I had been caught with a little under an ounce of crack cocaine. They gave me six months. I finally had made it to juvenile prison. That was one of the craziest experiences I ever had as a teenager

Samuel Woods

Chapter 6: Down Hill

I was sent to Circleville first for about 30 days while I waited for a transfer to my main facility. Circleville had about seven different dorms, all named after trees. You had Elm, which is where 12 years or younger boys were housed. There were also Hickory, Maple, Oak, and other tree named dorms. I landed in Hickory. The block was full of black kids. There were only 15 to 20 white boys and about 80 black boys. There was an upstairs and a downstairs, which they called tiers, and two wings in each block that held 20 juveniles on the bottom and top. About five tables sat in the pod area where you could sit and play cards, bones, and chess when we had inside rec. The CO's desk sat in the center of the block so they could see both sides of the whole block.

As you can imagine, there were lots of fights, and I got into my fair share. I used to hear stories about how niggas would try to play you. You had to fight, or you would get played like a bitch, and your time there would be hard, so I considered that. I already had my mind made up that I wasn't even going to play around. In the first situation I got into, I would beat my opponent up without hesitation.

I was still salty that I was in this situation in the first place, but I stayed focused on everything around me. Being in Circleville reminded me of our detention center. They used to do things military style. We would wake up around 5:30 am and walk to chow. We had to walk single file and had to recite a military cadence, left-right-left, left-right-left, as we walked to the chow hall, which was kind of far from our housing unit. Circleville was big as fuck, and you saw different blocks walking to and from chow. The blocks wore different colored sweaters with a matching stripe going down the side of the pants. Hickory wore orange. Maple wore purple, Elm green, and so on. When we made it to the chow hall, we only had a certain amount of time to eat. After the last person sat down with his tray of food, your time started. We got about five minutes total to eat. You would get into trouble if you held up the line, or you didn't get up from your seat fast enough. I couldn't wait to get to my main facility because I hated that when one person got into trouble, it cost all of us. They used to make us sit in plastic chairs for long periods. All they gave us was a book to read. We got one hour out of our cells for TV time.

One time, I had got into it with this other kid from Cleveland. Cleveland niggas used to think they were the shit. It was 1999, so I knew a lot these niggas didn't know too much of anything. We ended up getting into an argument about something. I don't remember what the beef was about, but I beat his ass. Everybody said I hit him with way more punches, but he was punching me hard. This young nigga hit like he was a grown man. It wasn't shit, though. I took the blows like they were soft as fuck. Later, we became good friends. We ended up going to the same facility. It was called *The Cuyahoga Hills* and was one of the roughest juvenile prisons in Ohio.

I was there holding it down. My nigga Tec was already there. He had been locked up for about five months already, so I was looking for him. I had to stay in the intake dorm for a couple of weeks, which was C- dorm. There were eight dorms with about 40 juveniles housed in each one. From the jump, I didn't like being in the hills due to the fact they treat you like you a kid. You couldn't do a lot of shit, and if one person talked when we were supposed to be on quiet time (QT), they would make you stand. They had us standing for hours and hours. I remember standing for at least three hours straight one time.

There were always fights; I mean all day every day. I had to fight a lot during my time at The Hills. I fought so much that I caught 30 extra days for excessive bad behavior. My first few months were the hardest because I always had to fight. There was always a kid who thought he was hard, and he would test my G, so I would beat him. I used to love to fight. I got a rush from fighting and beating whoever I fought.

I moved from C- dorm to G-dorm. I was the youngest one on the block, yet I was the most active. I stayed fighting. I always got into it with somebody because I felt like if I had to stand for you, then I didn't like you. If we had to keep rising because some dude couldn't shut up or whatever, I would fight him. All the CO's knew me for my fighting skills and gave me respect, just like the other juveniles did. There were a few niggas in there that knew how to fight and were beating niggas up as well. We used to be cool. I guess you can say we stayed out of each other's way because we never even got into an argument.

We had some mean-ass CO's that used to work on our block. CO Page used to beat your ass if you disrespected him. He would take you inside the box and fight you head up. He gave us fair ones. The box was like the hole. The box is where you would go when you got into a fight with other inmates or with any staff member. It was always cold as hell in the box, and they didn't have anything to sit on. You had to lay on the concrete floor, and sometimes you sat in there for hours at a time. I stayed inside the box because I was always in trouble, mainly for fighting. Mr. Johnson always would beat your ass, but he mostly slapped you right on the spot and called you all types of names, like bitch ass nigga, while he slapped you. He was crazy. I never got slapped by a CO. I think they knew I wasn't going for that, but Mr. Johnson made me stand for about five hours one time. And there was Mr. Good. Mr. Good was a big as fuck black nigga who used to walk around while we were standing, and if you kept talking or anything, he would slap you in the back of your head hard. The slap would be so loud that it would echo throughout the dorm.

I used to run into Tec going to and from the chow hall. He was on the other side of the prison in E dorm. That side held E thru H, and the side I was in held A thru D. H dorm was probably the coolest block because the CO's on that block didn't care what you did. Most of the juveniles in the block were serving years or even juvie life, meaning they weren't going home until they turned 21. I used to love going to the box in that dorm because Lou, the CO who had the block, used to let those niggas sit around playing music and kicking it. I never used to be in the box when I was over there. When I was serving my six months there, I didn't learn anything. I couldn't wait until I got home to go right back to the hood and resume where I left off. I was thinking of better ways to sell drugs. I never thought about changing or trying to stay out of the streets. The streets were forming me into a man at the time I took care of my mother, and I was putting things together.

Things for me started getting challenging after I was released. I was dealing with a few females at the same time. My daughter's mom was one of them. We used to post on the block and make sales together, and then she stole $600 from me when I took a trip to Columbus.

I knew something wasn't right before I got back because she wasn't returning any of my calls, nor was she calling me. As soon as I got back from Columbus, I went straight to my stash spot and saw my shit was missing, so I called and called her back to back. No answer. I went to my Uncle Warren's house to see if he or my cousin Mike had seen her. They both said no. I had Mike's baby momma take me over to her friend's house, who lived in the hood. I wanted her to fight her for stealing my money, but I knew she wouldn't because my daughter's mom had work. She knew how to fight, and everybody knew it.

When we pulled up to her friend's house, I asked her, "Aye, you trying to make a $100 real quick?" and reached into my pocket to retrieve the money.

"Doing what?" she replied.

"You trying to beat this bitch up real quick for me?" I said, looking serious so she would know I wasn't playing.

"Who?"

I said my baby mom's name, and she was like, "Hell nah, nigga. You tripping." She couldn't believe I was asking her to fight her for me. I knew she probably wouldn't, although she wasn't even pregnant by me, yet she was scared for real, so I just got out of the car. I went to her friend's door and knocked like I was the police.

"Who it is?" she yelled from the other side of the door

"It's me," and I said my nickname. She quickly opened the door.

"What's up, boy?" she said.

"Shit, where yo friend at?" I snarled.

"I don't know. I haven't seen her since, like, Saturday."

"Damn, since Saturday?" It was Monday, but I didn't know when she took the money. "Okay, Saturday. Where you see her at?"

"Man," she said, "I seen her at the bar."

"At the bar, oh yea?" I said, but I was thinking *What the fuck is yo ass doing at the muthafucking bar.*

"Why? What's up?"

I went ahead and told her, "Yo girl stole my money."

"Whatttttt?" was all she could say with a look of disbelief.

I knew she couldn't believe her girl stole my money, me of all people.

"Okay, ohhhh…that's how she was buying everybody drinks an' shit."

"Whatttttt? Wait a minute. She was buying muthafuckas drinks wit my money?"

"Ummhmmm, sho was, like she was ballin' or something."

Damn, I thought to myself. I couldn't believe how she had done me. We were just posted up on the block getting money together. I would give her anything she needed, so I didn't understand why she would steal from me.

"Okay, listen. This is what we gonna do. I want you to call her and tell her to come over…"

Before I could continue, she cut me off. "Nah, nah, wait a minute. I'm not getting in nothing y'all got going on."

When she said that I knew she was gonna try to play hardball, so I had something up my sleeve. One of my boys just given me about 30 ecstasy pills, and I knew that's what she and my girl used to do.

"Man, fuck all that. She stole. I know you ain't have nothing to do with it, but you just as guilty now because you drunk my money too. You just said she was buying you drinks. Come on now," I said, trying to make her feel bad. "Anyway, look, I got something for you. Come through for me."

"What you got?" she asked.

I reached in my pocket and pulled out the pills. "I got these Ex pills. What's up? I know you love these. Look, I'm a give you five of these. Just call me when she get here, alright?

"Okay, I got you. I got you."

"For real, don't play with my shit," I said. I looked directly into her eyes, so she would know I wasn't playing.

"Come on now. You know I ain't gonna play with yo shit. I got you. I'm a call you soon as she get here," she said.

I knew she wasn't playing, so I went back to my uncle's house. He lived right down the street. About 30 minutes later, she called and said my baby momma was there. I flew over there so fast. She must have seen me pull up because something told me to walk straight to the back door. There she was trying to run out the back.

"Where the fuck you going? Fuck is my money?" I asked angrier. I couldn't believe she was trying to sneak away. That was how I knew she stole from me.

"Baby, listen, this nigga robbed me."

"Man, you hear this shit?" I couldn't believe she would even try to hit me with that weak ass line. I felt so disrespected. I don't know what came over me, but I just reached back and slapped her in the mouth. Pooowwwwwww!

"Stop lying, bitch!" I said as I stepped back and dodged the windmill of punches and slaps she threw wildly at me. She was surprised I had smacked her, but I was even more surprised than she was. I never thought I would hit a female, especially after watching my mother being physically abused for so many years. She had taught me never to put my hands on a female, but she was serving me with the utmost disrespect. I couldn't believe she would even treat me like this. She didn't stop swinging at me, and then she caught me on my nose, which triggered my anger. I just started smacking her repeatedly. I slapped her until she fell to the ground. She was crying and screaming as loud as hell. By this time, it seemed like the whole hood was standing around now. I could hear people saying, "Okay, that's enough, bro. Chill! Chill!"

"I'm sending you to jail, nigga. You going to jail for putting yo hands on me," she yelled, but I didn't care about none of that shit she was talking about. I was only 17, so I didn't think I could catch a domestic violence charge.

"Bitch, call the police. I don't give a fuck, bitch! Get my money, you scandalous ass hoe!" I yelled in her ear so she could hear everything I said and know that the shit she had done wasn't right at all.

I walked off after that, still not understanding why she would steal the money. She knew that I would have given her some money if she needed it, but that wasn't the case. She wanted to betray my trust. It was cool because it was her loss.

About three hours later, I was posted on the block, and my mother called me, cussing me out. All I heard was, "You know better. I didn't raise you like that. You seen what I went through. You wrong, Sam. You dead wrong. Call that girl and apologize. You know damn well you ain't pose to be putting yo hands-on no woman, boy."

My mom dug in me for real, but I don't think she understood or knew what had happened. My mom asked me why I hit her, and I told her what happened. Then, she was mad at my girl, but she still felt like I should not have done that.

Truthfully, I felt terrible afterward. I had never hit a woman

Imprisonment

before that day. She had me doing things outside of my character. I regretted hitting her, especially a few months later when she told me she was pregnant. I didn't believe I was the father due to the fact we hadn't been together for months prior, so right before I went back to juvenile prison, and I didn't talk to her to find out the truth.

I was back in the hills doing only three months this time for another dope case. I didn't have to fight as much because many of the CO's and juveniles remembered me. I knocked out those three months like it was nothing. I got released and went right back to the street life, right back to the block hanging around the same dudes I had been around since I was 11 or 12 years old.

They were on the same shit, selling dope and gang banging. Nothing positive was coming from anybody I hung around, so there was only one thing that was going to go with that, getting locked up again.

I turned 18 in June of 2001 and was hit with another pregnancy. My son's mother was pregnant, and my daughter's mom had already had her, but I only held my baby girl one time. There was a big debate about whether she was mine, but I was with my son's mother at the time. When I found out that my son's mother was pregnant with him, I knew I had to get some money real fast. I was back selling dope, but the money was coming slowly. The hood wasn't jumping like before. I think the fiends were scared to come to the hood because the summer of 2001 was wild. The block kept getting shot up. I needed some quick cash, and I couldn't be waiting around for anybody to give me a handout.

Penitentiary chances are taken on the daily on the streets. There are all kinds of ways that one tries to get paid, most of them illegal. Trying to fend for yourself and your family gets hard at times. The struggle is real. I know what you're thinking. Why didn't I get a job? Getting a job is hard for somebody that's been selling drugs since he was 13 years old. It's hard to change his thinking when all he has known how to do is peddle drugs, so getting a job never crossed my mind when I came into a hard place. I did what you would say the dumbest shit ever, and it cost me ten years of my kids' life. Getting rehabilitated in prison isn't as easy as they try to make it seem.

Samuel Woods

Chapter 7: Hard Time

When I first arrived at County, I was full of frustration. I didn't want to be there knowing that I wasn't going to be getting back out to the streets for some time. I was in there for a carrying a concealed weapon. I had been pulled over with one of my boys and a couple of females when they found a gun.

When I went to my first court date to see if I was going to get a bond, a detective came to speak to me about a robbery. As soon as I got back to the county, I was charged with that robbery. I couldn't believe it. To make things worse, the county was dirty and wasn't even that big. It was overcrowded and full of dope fiends. I was placed in C1 south, which was the felony pod. People with F1's thru F3's were on this pod, a lot of 18-year-olds like me.

I wore a chip on my shoulder, so I fought constantly during the six months I was there. I hated the county, and I couldn't wait to leave after sentencing. You might think it was strange for someone to be in a hurry to get prison, but if you spent one week in Stark County, you would see why.

The food was horrible, but it's not only that. They fed you the same things every week. Monday for breakfast, you get some super watered-down oatmeal, two pieces of bread, and two cartons of milk. Tuesday was two hard-boiled eggs with two slices of bread and two small containers of milk. On Wednesdays, you may get two pancakes that were either burnt or not cooked thoroughly with the same watered-down oatmeal. The food is cold most of the time. You may get cold cereal one day, and the lunches were even worse. They served one piece of baloney with black eye peas just about every other day. I hated that food. I never ate that stuff unless I was in the hole and didn't have a choice. Usually, I ate chips or candy bars from the commissary. They allow you to spend only $40 a week, $30 on food, and $10 on hygiene. It was pure torture for me. They only give you one sheet and two blankets so thin you can see through them. You can only imagine how cold I was since it was winter.

I used to freeze my ass off. They had us in single-man cells, 16 inmates to a range. On each block, the dorms were different. I spent time in them also, and I was happy to be in the cell blocks. In those dorms, it was so packed they had me sleeping on a boat, which is like a hard, plastic boat-shaped bed on the floor. You get a mat to put on top of it, and that's where you'd sleep on the floor. They only had two toilets that sat right next to each other, so if you had to take a shit and somebody else did too at the same time, you would be sitting right next to each other stinking up the whole dorm.

They had two TVs in the block, one on each side of the block. The block is divided in half, cells one through eight on one side of the gate, and nine through 16 on the other side. There was one TV on the nine through 16 end and another on the one through eight side. A TV hung on the wall opposite the bars that separated the walls and windows from the cells. There was no remote, probably because there were too many fights over it. We had to make a remote by rolling up a bunch of writing paper until it was long and hard enough not to bend you push it against the buttons on the TV. We would place an eraser from a pencil on the end to help with turning the TV.

I hated being in the county. All-day, every day, you heard guys talking about their cases. Every last one said the same thing, "I didn't do it." "I'm innocent." "I wasn't there. They got the wrong person." And then you would read the evidence they had against them and see that their asses were guilty as hell. All the evidence would point right at them, and they would still sit there and say, "It wasn't me." Then you had some who were snitching in their case. You knew who the snitches were because they never wanted to talk about their cases. They were quiet. You would find everything out about them when you went to court with them. Most of the guys in there would take a deal so they wouldn't have to go to trial and get more time. That's all I saw my whole six months, guys taking deals. I did not take my six-year deal and going to trial cost me as far as how much time the judge was going to give me.

Imprisonment

It was evident that I would be sent to prison someday. Given the lifestyle I lived, it was either that or death. It was almost like I didn't care if I lived or died or stayed a free man. I didn't realize the severity of living life in general. I lived day to day without a purpose, with no sense of direction. I didn't have a reason for my life, so how could I care about my life or my family or the kids I made? Prison destined for me. I wasn't surprised that I was sitting in the county facing robbery and gun charges only a couple of months after my 18th birthday.

Back then, you would get a direct indictment, meaning I was indicted within the first week without any evidence or anything. I sat in the county for about a month before I was appointed a lawyer by the state, which is what they do when you can't afford a paid lawyer to represent you at court. They appointed Wayne Graham Jr. to my case. I went from a CCW charge to an armed robbery. When I went to court for the gun charge, a detective who came to interview me said a man name John Lennard was accusing me of robbing him. Now, this is where my life got real.

I sat in the county stressing because I didn't know what was about to happen to me. It took about 2 ½ months before I got my motion of discovery. Discovery contains everything from your indictment, including statements made by anybody involved in the case and all the evidence against you. After I got that, I was able to see what the fuck was going on. I saw this nigga was trying to get me sent to prison for a robbery. I was sticking to my innocence so much that I went to trial.

My first visit from Wayne Graham Jr. was horrible. Right off the bat, he was against me. He tried to tell me everything that wasn't getting me home and out of this situation. He kept saying things like, "Do you think the jury is going to believe you?" I swear he was never working for me at all. He didn't care about me saying I didn't commit this robbery or that I didn't know who did. He didn't care about any of that. All he cared about was me taking a 6-year deal that the judge told him to negotiate with me. They had decided I was guilty. It felt like anybody could say you did something, and they would believe them even with no evidence backing the story. Since I didn't have a paid lawyer, I was in this fight alone. My lawyer never worked for me even though he was appointed to me by the court. He had been sent to get me to take a deal. That's how the courts work in Stark County. Their main objective is to get you to take a deal, so they don't have to pay for trial expenses.

They don't care whether you are innocent; they want to get the guilty plea and the money for sending you to prison. I had to learn about the system. I was blind to a lot of things dealing with the court system.

I was not accepting the way my lawyer tried to play me, so I decided against the deal the judge offered me and made them go to trial. My attorney said the judge wanted me to take six years. I was like, "Fuck that! Six years for what? Some nigga who lied in the first place, talking 'bout he got robbed for some money and showed the cops some pay stubs he had from some weak ass blood bank job he had? Yea, okay."

The trial didn't last long. My lawyer didn't put up a fight. It was like he didn't even want to win, let alone try. I was 18, so knowing how to handle that whole situation was hard for me. I didn't have any older homies to go to for advice. I had no nobody there for me. I was all alone in that courtroom. My trial lasted one day, and I got sentenced a few weeks later. Walking into the courtroom shackled from my hands to my feet, made me feel like a slave. I had so much anger inside of me. It was unbearable. I couldn't even look my mother in her face as she stared at me, wishing she could do something to get me out of this harsh situation. I was facing ten years as my maximum sentence. After I went to trial and lost, I found out the truth. The dude had dope cases pending, so to clear those charges up, he took the stand, lied like he was a victim when he was just as much of a criminal as I was.

"Will the court stand for Honorable Judge John Hass?" the bailiff said. Everybody stood up as he stepped out from the back. I was looking at him with anger in my eyes. I hated him. He didn't care about anybody's life, and I hated that fact. Now he had my future in his hands. I didn't trust him to do the right thing. He was old with a head full of white hair. He didn't look at me one time. I could tell he wasn't fond of blacks. It showed in his demeanor.

"Okay, we are here today for the sentencing of Mr. Samuel Woods. At this time, does the defendant have anything they wish to say?"

When the judge said that, my snake ass lawyer leaned over to me and asked if I wanted to say something. I quickly stood up.

"Yes, your honor, I just want to say I'm innocent, and I had nothing to do with this robbery," I said that looking at him right in his eyes. Then I sat down. I already knew it didn't matter what I said. He already had made up his mind.

"Okay, Mr. Woods, the court had the chance to hear you speak, but I have to say you act like rules don't apply to you. I know you said you are innocent, but here it is, the jury found you guilty. I don't think you understand the crime you committed here was a serious offense, and for that, I'm going to have to give you the maximum sentence of ten years."

As soon as he said that, I heard my mom scream, "Oh Lord!" It was loud as hell and made me turn around. She started crying. It made me sad to see her like that. I still was standing, but I was still looking at the judge's face. He couldn't look at me, though. It didn't hit me that I had been sentenced to a decade until I reached my parent institution.

Before I walked out of the courtroom, my mom yelled, "Stay strong, son. You okay. You will be home. I love you."

I yelled, "I love you." Then, I exited the courtroom. My mind was on some other shit. I was mad as fuck, but it was nothing I could do. I knew I had to do every day of those ten years. I thought to myself, *Damn, ten years. For what?*

Samuel Woods

Chapter 8: Freedom Stricken

Chained and shackled like a runaway slave, I tried to peek through the cracks of the sealed off windows of the bluebird to see the road and cars we passed on my way to prison. The bus was full; 75% of us on the bus were black, about 15% were white, and the other 10% was Spanish. We were all going to Lorain Correctional Prison, the intake facility where you go to wait until a bed opens for you at the institution where you will serve your sentence.

Lorain was no cakewalk. As soon we arrived, we came across this CO who looked Chinese. He was a straight asshole, a bonafide dick. We didn't even step off the bus before he started yelling and getting all in our faces. I guess he was trying to scare us because a lot of us were young.

"Get your fucking asses lined up, you stupid muthafuckas. You in my house now, muthafuckas. You hear me? My house and I make the rules in this bitch! And you muthafuckas is gonna follow my muthafuckin' rules, or it's gonna be consequences. Now, face the wall, muthafuckas! All of you muthafuckas put yo muthafuckin' face toward that wall."

Dude was crazy. A little chubby old man that probably couldn't take one punch to the chin talking all this shit was funny to me, but I wasn't laughing. My ass was facing that wall. It was late December, so it was cold as hell. We didn't have coats or anything on, and I just was wondering why the hell he had us standing outside in the cold. That shit made me mad as fuck, but I stood there facing the wall, not saying anything. After standing outside for about 20 minutes, they started calling us in one by one as he read our names off a list.

"When I yell yo name, step back and walk into that door."

He was calling names in alphabetical order, so I was going to be last due to my last name being Woods. I was pissed. My name was the last one he called. When I stepped into the door, they had me walk into a small room where he took off our cuffs. Twenty-three or 24 men were in a circle inside this tiny room standing shoulder-to-shoulder. The next thing I knew, a 6'6" lumberjack-looking dude walked in and started talking crazy to us.

"Alright, you sons of bitches, listen up because I'm not about to be repeating myself. You gonna strip naked…"

All I heard was, "What? Come on, man."

"Shut the fuck up! I don't give a fuck about what the fuck you guys crying about. You gonna take that fucking jumpsuit off, or I'll take the muthafucker off myself — Yo fucking choice. Don't matter to me. Now shut the fuck up and listen!" He was pissed. I could tell by the way his tone changed.

"Now, like I said, you gonna take everything the fuck off right here right now!"

I guess nobody was moving, so he yelled from the top of his lungs, "I SAID TAKE THAT SHIT OFF RIGHT FUCKING NOW. FUCK IS Y'ALL WAITING FOR!"

We striped to our bare nakedness fast. We were standing there freezing our asses off.

"Now, one by one, y'all put everything in the bag that's sitting on the ground behind you from the jumpsuit to your fucking socks. You got it?"

We did what he said. Then we had to stand back facing the wall asshole naked. I could hear the Chinese man outside the room talking shit. He was saying stuff like, "Make them stand in there for 30 minutes. Fuck them muthafuckas. Freeze them to death." The next thing I knew, he walked into the room, clowning and talking shit.

"Look at you stupid muthafuckas standing in a small ass room asshole naked. Look at y'all li'l dicks all balled up. Don't you muthafuckas feel stupid? This is the way you muthafuckas want to live, huh? Stupid pieces of shit. I will never have respect for you dummies. Fuck you, muthafuckas. I hate you muthafuckas. Why should I care about you when you don't even give a fuck about yourselves?"

Damn, I thought, *he saying some crazy shit*. Still, he was saying some shit that I know had all of us thinking.

"Now, you muthafuckas, listen up. We gotta check you muthafuckas for drugs, weapons. Shit, we don't know what you muthafuckas may or may not try. I've seen some crazy shit in my years working here, so we gonna walk up to you guys one by one. All you stupid muthafuckas have to do is listen. That's it. You got it."

He started walking up to each of us going around one side of the room, the other tall guy on the other side said, "Alright, turn around. Lift your arms in the air. Lift up yo nut sack. Turn around. Bend over and cough. Lift your right foot up, now your left foot. Alright, get yo ass back in line."

I felt so violated, and it was the worst feeling standing there, letting some other guy look all over my body. That shit made me feel nasty as fuck. I hated standing next to another man bare naked, but I remained focused. After we were done with all that, we got some whites to wear and then another jumpsuit, which was green. Then they put us in another small ass room with I sink and toilet that was hooked together. We were so packed together we could barely move. It didn't make any sense. Four hours had passed since we arrived. They gave a brown paper bag with two peanut butter and jelly sandwiches one apple. They read off names again, and of course, I was last. When your name was read, you went and talked to some lady to verify that you were the person they had on the paper. Then they put you into another room where you would wait to be called to yet another room, and then they sent you off to another area at the facility.

This is where you would get your hair cut bald, and you would be ready to go to the block where you would be housed. They put me in 4A, which was the block for 18 to 23-year-olds. It was off the chain with a lot of fighting and getting into it with the CO's. I ran into a lot of dudes I had met in juvie. I couldn't believe how many of us had graduated from juvenile prison to the real prison in such a short time.

The block was mostly black males. You didn't see many whites or even Spanish guys housed in the block. There were about 120 of us all together with two inmates to each cell. The cell was so small you could barely move. It was very stressful. You had no TV in the cell, but you could buy a Sony FM radio from the commissary for about $23. They were getting over on us, and it was hard to find reception in those cells as well. The food wasn't that much better than the food they served us in county jail, and I hated eating that too. The trays were always dirty, and the kitchen had a weird smell. We had to walk in a single file line there also. They made you go to every chow. It didn't matter if you had commissary in your box or not. They gave you one hour of rec every day sometimes one day outside and another day inside.

There wasn't anything to do inside rec but play cards, watch TV in the TV room, and use the phones. That was the only time you could make calls besides when they went from cell to cell, letting you and your cellmate out for one 15-minute call, which wasn't every day. We used the phone maybe three times a week. In 2001, they still had tobacco products in prison, so we smoked, played cards, and listened to the radio all day. Lorain was so boring. I hated it. It felt like we were locked down all the time with nothing to do.

I couldn't stop thinking about my son. My son was born on December 19th, and I still hadn't seen him. I'd received some photos of him, but pictures weren't like having him in my arms for the first time. I was so happy when I first received the pictures. It was after I been in Lorain for a couple of months. I had to have my mother and my son's mother get approved to visit me before I could see them. After that process was over and done with, they set up a visit. So, after three long months of me waiting to see my son, it happened. I was so happy, beyond happy. I thought he was long as hell. He slept through almost the whole visit, but just holding him and finally being able to kiss him gave me the best feeling in the world. I was hurt that it had to be like this; my first time seeing and holding my son was inside a prison visitation room.

A week or so after seeing my son, I was sent to my parent institution, which was Trumbull Correctional, a level three prison. A lot of violent offenders were there as opposed to guys who have drug charges, who usually go to a lower level like a one or a two. I would spend four and a half years there before I moving to a level four for an assault on another inmate. My stay at Trumbull consisted of fighting and fighting and more fighting. I used to kick guys' boxes, only white guys boxes. Kicking boxes meant that I would walk into another inmate's cell and open their box and take all their food or anything valuable.

I was bad, and I didn't care. I had no regard for anybody else around me. I wasn't trying to learn a thing that first couple of years in prison. I still was numb to being handed ten years. I was mad at the world. My family tried to be there for me, but they were struggling on the outside. I had to fend for myself. I hated the white boys. I thought I'd make them pay for the judge, lawyer, and prosecutor putting it down on me, so I took them through hell. I took their shit every chance I got and didn't care anything about how anyone felt about it.

As I got into doing my ten-year sentence, I began to learn a lot about the underworld of prison. I stayed in the hole for all types of reasons. Most of the time, it was because I was fighting or a cussing out a CO. I had no respect for the CO's I hated them just like they hated us. To me, all CO's hated inmates, and they showed it by treating us like shit. They talked to us like we we're the scum of the earth. For that and many other reasons, I was rebellious. I had no thoughts or feelings or plans or anything dealing with wanting to change to try and become a better person, and the prison didn't offer anything either. I was trapped inside the belly of the beast, being eaten alive and didn't even know it. I was blind the whole time to the existence of oneself and transformation to be a different person. I was caught in the web, the web of the prison politics and the underworld life.

Samuel Woods

Chapter 9: Bossman

It was 2004 going on my 3rd year since I was found guilty at my trial for aggravated robbery. I was about to turn 21 years old. I was still so young, but I felt older than my years, and I carried myself as such.

I had been released from the hole for a disrespect ticket I caught in another block when I was moved into a cell with this guy named Bossman. Bossman wasn't your average person. He was somebody in the prison world, but at the time I didn't know just how much power one man could have in a place where we were the ones who were supposed to be getting told what to do. Yet it was him telling people what to do, even CO's. He lived up to his name in every sense of the word. My time in prison took a drastic turn for the better and then for the worse.

"What's up?" I said as I sat all my things down on the floor next to the bunk.

"What up?" he responded as he stared at me.

"I'm Ohle."

"I know who you are. Call me Bossman. Get yo shit together. We a talk later, alright."

"Alright," I spat back. *Damn*, I thought to myself, *He's a real player*. I could tell he was somebody just by the way he talked. He had a lot of confidence. I couldn't wait until later when we could talk.

That whole day all my guys told me how lucky I was to be in Bossman's cell and how I was about to be cool in there. They were saying all types of shit. They had me curious as to what the fuck they all were talking about.

I housed in 13 East, which at that time was the most violent block in the whole prison. It was wild and full of young inmates who didn't have much to care for, so there were lots of fights daily. I felt right at home. It was my type of environment.

We finally were locked down for the night, and I was anxious to talk with Bossman. I just felt like he was about to give me some of that game I was needing.

"What's up, Ohle? You know who I am, don't you?"

I said yea, but the truth was I just got familiar with him since I been in the block.

"Heard you got a picture with me in it."

"I do?" I responded, confused.

"You got some pictures Spider sent you when he got out, right?"

"Oh, yea. Damn, you had me thinking like what the hell he talking 'bout?" We both laughed as I dug through my pictures and found the photo with him in it. He quickly picked himself out as he showed me, and it was sure enough him. He looked the same, and it was like we got tight off that alone. We talked for hours that night, nothing too deep. It was more like he was trying to find out what type of shit I was on. He told me that I should stop kicking boxes said there would be no need for that.

"Nothing good comes from stealing," Bossman said.

He told me I needed to leave that part of my bidding behind, so that's what I did. Bossman showed me a lot and taught me a lot, as well. I mean, I didn't know anything about the underworld in prison. He gave me the game. One day I walked into the cell, and he asked, "How much money you got on your books?"

"I got like $200. Why? What's up?" I replied.

He didn't say anything, just gave me a look then left the cell. I knew he was pushing, but I never saw anything. That night he broke everything down to me. He told me that we weren't going to play any games. He told me to get my money and said he was going to have me spend that money at the store so he could load the cell up with food. He gave me ten grams the next day. Ten grams of powder were now in my possession. I didn't know what to say, but I was happy because I knew I was about to make some money. I would make no less than $1,500, but I didn't make that much because I was looking out for all my homies from my city and my hood. Bossman was angry with me for that. Now, I understand why, but back then, I didn't. I was only 20 years old, so I didn't know any better. I didn't have that proper understanding of getting yourself on your own feet before you go and put somebody else on theirs. And that's what he told me.

He said, "Listen, Ohle. You tripping, Brah. I understand you want to look out for yo niggas, but how can you do that when you ain't even got yourself right yet?"

The shit he was saying was making so much sense. "You right, Boss. I'm trippin'. I got you, though, my nigga." I replied with confidence thinking about how I'm a hustle the next bag. During my time in the cell with Bossman, he used to get pictures of different houses he said he owned. He had something going on where he was buying homes like crazy. Years later, I found out he was running a scam, and he hit the banks for 1.6 million dollars. He was the coldest. He made $1.6 million behind prison walls. If that ain't a hustler, then what do you call that? He only had to do two more years for that crime.

Now, I wasn't the one to be all in someone's business, so I never asked him how he was doing what he was doing. Still, being in that cell with him, I saw so many things that I never knew or even thought I would see inside a prison. I saw pounds of weed, ounces of cocaine, crack cocaine, and heroin. Bossman had the whole prison in his pocket. He ran Trumbull, and I was right there in the middle of it all.

One night we drank real liquor. He handed me a cup that had Hennessey inside of it. We got so drunk that night. I couldn't believe I was drinking real alcohol while watching him snort line after line of coke. He loved that coke. My time in that cell with Bossman was the best. I made so much money, and I got so much game from him. I used to try to pick his brain every chance I got. He was the talk of the prison. All the CO's and staff knew he flooded the jail with drugs, but nobody could prove it. Nobody knew how he was getting the drugs into the prison, not even me, and I celled with him for four months. He was one of the rawest hustlers I had ever seen in prison. I still haven't met anyone that could fuck with my cousin. That nigga had yachts and everything. When the Feds finally got him, they found $600 thousand and a brick of cocaine. They also found another brick on his yacht, but they didn't have a warrant for that, so they had to throw it out. He ended up doing 15 years in the feds, but as far as knowing anyone who could fuck with his hustle, no one came close.

I thought about how I was going to move the next time. It felt good to be able to send money home to my son that I left out there alone. I had gotten back on my feet this time. I had some green too, and I was moving it real fast. I pushed it, and the soft went quickly as well. Everything was going well for my squad and me. Then, as the saying goes, all good things must come to an end.

Just like that, my run was over. I ended up getting caught up in some bullshit fucking with one of my niggas from Cleveland. They called him Black Crook. Days before this, he kept telling me that he wanted to take the white boy's velour blanket and fan.

"Why, Brah? You got your own velour and a fan. You trippin', Brah," I replied.

"I don't like that dude. He think he can't be touched, man. I'm taking his shit. Fuck him!"

"Nah, Brah, fuck that shit. We over here chilling, getting money. We don't need all that," I said to Crook.

I thought what I was saying started to make sense to him because he said, "You right. You right."

A few days go by, and that nigga Crook went up in that white boy's cell and took all his shit. I just knew some bullshit was about to happen because the white boy was an Aryan Brother (AB). He was in that white supremacist shit. They hate blacks and Latinos or whatever. All the homies were on Crook's chest about him taking the white boy's shit after we sat there and told his ass not to do it, but he didn't care at all. And just like I thought, it happened.

I was upstairs in one of the homies from the city's cell. We were smoking some weed when I heard a loud ding noise like a piece of metal hit metal. Then I heard a bunch of squeaking noise like somebody was fighting. When I looked out the cell window, I saw my nigga Rob squaring up with one of the white boys. He had a pipe in his hand. He hit the white boy with a two-piece and dropped him. The pipe fell as well. Then my nigga went upstairs as I ran to my nigga cell. I had my shower shoes on, so I had to kick them off and put his shoes on, which I couldn't even fit.

I put them on anyway, and I ran out the cell right into my nigga Big Kev and the white boy whose cell Crook robbed. They were fighting over the pipe. I guess Big Kev caught it when he tried to hit him with it.

"Ohle, get this muthafucka!" Kev yelled.

With no hesitation, I punched the white boy as hard as could. I had aimed for the side of his face, but he turned, so that's where my punch landed. He fell from the impact. Kev was able to get full control of the pipe. He then went crazy, chasing any and all white boys down, hitting them with the pipe.

The CO's were running around, trying to cuff up the ones they saw with pipes or fighting. I then ran to assist another one of my guys, and I hit this other white boy in his chin. He took off running after I did that, but after I hit him, my hand felt funny. By this time, a gang of CO's was in the block, locking us down. While we were all locked down, my hand started to throb. It began to swell, too. I knew it was broken. Bossman let me have it.

"Man, you stupid as fuck, Ohle. Why the fuck yo ass get involved in that dumb shit? I told you that stealing shit don't bring nothing but problems that a nigga don't need. Now look, you 'bout to go to the hole for what and you done broke yo hand." He was shaking his head back and forth in disbelief.

"Man, Ohle, I'm disappointed in you, man. I can't believe you, Brah. You got shit going on, man. Them dumb niggas ain't got shit going on. Now, you might ride out, stupid."

He made me feel worse than I already did. I knew I had made a dumb decision by getting involved in that shit, but I had a problem with being loyal. When I fuck with you, I fuck with you. My loyalty was always my downfall. They were going cell to cell checking hands, and I knew once they got to my cell that I was going down. They came and saw how swollen my hand was, and they knew I had been fighting. They cuffed me up, and I spent about 45 days in the hole. They ended up riding the white boys out instead of us because they had sawed the bars off that were connected to under the bunks and turned them into pipes to use as weapons. That was the only reason we made it out of that situation without having to ride out.

After I was released, I went to a couple of blocks and bounced around for over a year, and then I ended up back on 13 East, the same block where I had broken my hand. It was hell getting my hand working right again. First, they didn't even put my cast on right. The bone that had broken didn't heal after those first eight weeks, so they put a pin in my hand, which was the most excruciating pain I had ever felt in my life. My hand was bent all up after I got the pin and the cast removed. I had to build the strength up in my hand by squeezing a little blue ball all day every day. I finally could move my hand and open it up straight all the way. And I was able to ball my fist back up. It took several months to get full use of my hand again, but I did. That was some the worst and hardest time of my ten years.

I ended up back on 13 East. Just like last time, it was a lot of guys from my city, but this time a lot of them were from my hood. My luck ran out. It was 2006, and things were alright. Time was flying. I was knocking those years out. Then I was hanging around a couple of my hood niggas. Things were going well for a few months; then, the li'l homie got into it with this big nigga from Warren. He was locked up for burning his girlfriend's nipples off with an iron, so not a lot of people fucked with him or liked him.

He and Narro got into it about a domino game. Narro said he caught the nigga trying to cheat, so he threw the dominoes in his face. The big nigga wanted some work, but he knew we weren't about to allow that. Narro pulled up on Tec and me and told us what happened. We then went downstairs to confront the sucker on it. He was talking strong, yelling, and trying to make a scene. I told that sucker to relax. I would beat his ass during the second shift when we get some cool CO's that wouldn't care if we fight, but he was just all talk. The second shift came, and he was ducking work, saying we were going to jump him. It was true, but how was he going to come out and say that?

The dude from Warren must have thought we were going to just let him talk shit and not do anything. While he was in the shower, a dude from my city named Art and I took everything from his cell, including all of his food. While we were doing that, I guess somebody must have given him a hint or something because he caught me coming out of the cell with a bunch of his shit. I knew somebody said something because he was dripping soaking wet with water. He never dried off, so I know he was alerted.

"What you got, man?" he said as I walked right past him.

"I ain't got shit," I replied, and I kept going toward the stairs. I saw him walking toward the CO's desk and point up toward me. As he was snitching on me, Tec came from behind him and punched him so hard his towel fell. It was a hard, loud punch. I heard it from way upstairs. I gave Art the shit I had on me, and I ran downstairs to assist my nigga. When I got there, they already were cuffing Tec up, so I just ran up on the sucker. He was ass hole naked. I just started punching on him, and he was trying to grab me. I was trying to avoid him because he was naked, but at the same time, I was trying to knock his ass out. He had me by my shirt hanging on for dear life. I could hear niggas in the background.

"Hit that nigga, Narro. Get 'em. Get that nigga off, Ohle."

I could feel Narro pulling him away. Narro had a tight grip on the sucker's neck. Narro fell back but still had him a headlock, so I went crazy on that sucker. I got to stomping and punching him all over. I was kicking him all in his head and everything, all while the CO was trying to stop me. He tried to grab me, but I pushed him off me. Then I just started kicking him right up between his ass like I was punting a football I was kicking him hard, fucking his ass up. You could hear everybody in the whole block laughing after I kicked him in his ass. He shook every time I kicked him. After I kicked him a good four times, more CO's ran into the block and snatched Narro and me up. They took us to the hole where we sat for seven months waiting to move to Lucasville, the roughest, dirtiest, and most fucked up prison in Ohio. It was a level four, where we would be locked down 23/7. That's when I had to grow up fast.

Samuel Woods

Imprisonment

Chapter 10: Solitary Confinement

We sat in the hole at Trumbull, waiting for beds to open. We did seven months, and all we heard was how fucked up Lucasville prison was. It was the worst, deadliest, roughest prison in Ohio. We heard so many stories. I am not going to lie. I did not want to go. Not only was it four or five hours away from my city, but all the CO's there were racist from what dudes that had done time there said. They told us stories about how they hated blacks and a lot of the hatred steamed from the 1993 riot that took place when multiple CO's and inmates were killed. They said that there were so many dead bodies piled on top of each other that they were finding people who weren't dead but on the verge of dying. They had been stabbed multiple times but survived. I guess this is why ever since then, Lucasville has been called the worst of all prisons in Ohio.

I arrived in Lucasville on September 28, 2006, when I was 23 years old. I had spent most of the time in the hole reading books and preparing myself for this trip. I had read more than 50 books, and I gained more mental strength as well as physical. I worked out daily, and I built on my mind more than anything. I wasn't your average 23-year-old. I thought differently than most. It was like all the game my older homies and uncles, and my older brother had shown me didn't hit me until I was 23 and on my way to one of the toughest prisons ever built. I had to get ready for this journey, and that's what I did. When I finally got to Lucasville, I was ready for whatever.

The bus ride to Lucasville wasn't like any bus ride I had ever experienced before. They had us chained up from our ankles around our waist, and then they had our hands cuffed inside this small black box that made your hands stack on top of each other. It is the most uncomfortable feeling I have ever felt in my life. I was so frustrated on the ride up to Lucasville. My ankles were bleeding from the tight shackles that sat right on the top of my bone. My chin was bleeding, and my hands were cramped up from the black box. An ex-prisoner invented the black box that twisted our hands. By the time I got to the maximum prison, I was exhausted and in pain. I was highly upset, and I didn't have room for any bullshit.

As we entered the prison, they took us straight to the medical area. I guess that's protocol. We walked down some of the longest hallways I had ever seen. We had to walk around metal detectors. They had metal detectors in every hall right before you reached the gate. The whole prison was controlled by the person who worked in the main booth. Every time you arrived at a barrier, he had to open it so you could walk through; Lucasville was locked down on deadbolt lock type shit.

After we sat in a cage for hours, the nurse took our vitals and asked us stupid ass questions like whether or not we have HIV or Hepatitis and when we last drank, smoked, or did drugs. It was around eight when I finally was being walked to the block where I was going to be sitting in the cell for seven months straight.

All kinds of thoughts ran through my mind as I stood outside the block, waiting for the door to slide open. As soon as it did, I heard guys yelling and screaming.

"Bitch, fuck you."

"Nah, fuck you, bitch! Suck my dick, you pussy."

I couldn't believe what I was hearing. Those types of words only meant one thing, and that was *I'm gonna try to kill you when I get the chance*. It was so dark I thought I was walking through a haunted house. In reality, I was. I was walking amongst the dead and the living dead.

As soon as I walked through the door, a CO stood waiting for me. There was another booth to my right with a CO inside it controlling the buttons of the gates. The smell of shit was so strong; it burned my nose. I had never smelled anything like it before in my life.

"Geez, Woods, I been waiting for you all day, man. Look, step up on that fourth step so I can get those shackles. Alright, man, here this is for you too." He handed me a bag with all kinds of food and sweets inside. There also was a CD player. The CO saw the look on my face and answered my unspoken question.

"This came from yo brother, Kev. He's next door on the other side."

"Oh, thank you," I said, surprised that a CO would be handing me a bag with food and all type of shit in it, a white CO at that. It fucked me up, but I kept my cool as I thought about my nigga Kev. I had to grab the bag in my cuffed hands. It was a small bag, but it still had some weight on it. I stepped up on the fourth steps as we walked through the gate. The steps were steel with holes going all through them. The entire prison seemed like it was all brick and metal. All of the cells were concrete from the ceiling to the floors. I had my bag gripped tight, so It wouldn't slip out of my hands as I walked. The smell of shit got worse as I reached the top of the steps, where there was another gate that had to be open before I entered the block that held some of the worst inmates in Ohio.

I was nervous as hell as I anticipated what was coming next. I still was hearing dudes call each other all types of crazy names saying all kinds of crazy shit to each other. When I heard somebody say *suck the skin off my dick, you fuck ass nigga*, I knew I had to get the fuck out of this prison as fast as possible. It felt like it took forever for the gate to slide open, but when it finally did, I didn't hesitate. I walked through it with my head held high, and my chest poked out. My face was twisted up crazy. I made sure I kept my eyes straight ahead. I wasn't trying to look in anybody's cell. I didn't know these niggas, and I wasn't trying to get to know any of them. We passed about six cells before we reached mine. You could hear the door slide open; it was loud as hell but not quite louder than the group of dudes yelling at each other. I dropped the bag on my mat and got the cuffs removed from my sore wrists, which had a deep mark from the handcuffs.

"Alright, Woods, good luck, Buddy. I'll let Kev know you here, and you got the bag. Talk to you later, man. Watch yourself, man. Watch yourself," he said before walking away.

It was so weird that he was so cool. I had heard tons of stories about how prejudiced the CO's were. It fucked me up, but I knew how my nigga Kev was. He probably had been giving these CO's hell, so they respected him.

My first night in Lucasville was crazy, but the worst part of my first night would have to be how nasty the cell they moved me in was. I had never seen anything so disgusting. I checked to make sure there wasn't any shit in my cell because of the smell. The filth and dried up dirt in the sink made me gag. I had to hold my breath.

It was so nasty I didn't want to touch anything in that cell. I then looked inside the toilet to discover an even more disgusting scene. There was a thick dark ring of piss around the inside of the toilet. It looked as if it had never been cleaned before. The stench of urine hit my nose hard. I was steaming. I couldn't believe that somebody was living under these conditions the shit was just horrible I mean I didn't know where to start, but I knew I had to get this shit cleaned up and cleaned up fast. I was so mad that I was there that I couldn't even think straight.

The cell was small and reminded me of being in the county because of the bars and the tiny part that slid open when they popped the door. I saw big ass TVs hanging on the wall as I looked through the bars, and there were windows, but all I could see was another cell block that sat across the yard. I could see the bars and everything right through the window, including the person who was in the cell. I stood there with my arms swinging through the bars, heart beating fast, and mind running crazy. I saw an inmate walking up the range through a small crack between the bars of my cell. The range was 20 cells long, which was long. It had 20 on the top and 20 on the bottom. The bottom level had more space; the top range tiny; you could almost touch the bars that blocked you from falling off the range onto the bottom level.

I caught a glimpse of somebody walking up the range. I couldn't wait until he reached my cell so that I could get some help. The guy was tall and big as fuck; I'm talking muscles everywhere. He happened to be walking to my cell anyway.

"You Ohle, right?" he said, looking like Michael Duncan. I mean, he looked like he could have been his twin brother for real. He was a little intimidating. By the way he talked and stood, you knew he wasn't the type of nigga to fuck with.

"Yea, what's up?"

"Your brothers next door told me to tell you to go to the vent so they can holla at you, and Kev want to make sure you got that shit he sent to you!"

"Oh, yea, tell him I got it. Good looking." I said. Then I asked what vent because I didn't see one in here besides the one above the door at the front of the cell.

"It's under that desk back there," he said, pointing. "He way down on the other end. You may not be able to hear him, but if you need anything, let me know, alright!"

I was so happy to hear him say that. "Hell yeah, I need some help. I need a broom and some cleaning supplies, a rag. I mean, I need all types of shit. Everything you got, man, please. It's so nasty in here. I can't sleep like this. Please tell me you got me. Uhhh!"

"Willy, my name Willy, and I do got you. Don't even trip. I'll be back. Hold up."

Just knowing I was about to be able to clean the cell made me feel a lot better. When Willy came back, he had a broom dustpan, a bottle of disinfectant, two pieces of a ripped up old shirt, and a pair of gloves. I couldn't wait to start cleaning.

"Aye, could you tell Kev I'm trying to clean this cell up. I'll talk to him when I'm done, alright?"

"Yea, I'll let him know. You gotta hurry up with that shit though because they 'bout to lock me down in like 15-20 minutes, alright?"

"Yea, I got you. Aye, do you know when they gonna bring my shit?"

"Ain't no telling, man. They don't do they job around here. This Luke, li'l brah. This the worst of the worst, for real."

As he walked away, I went straight to that toilet and got busy. It took a little longer than 30 minutes to finish cleaning the cell. They had taken the cleaning supplies away from me, but Willy gave me a jar filled with disinfectant so I could finish wiping everything down. The cell smelled and looked much better when I was done; it still felt dirty to me, though.

After I finished cleaning, I went to the vent. I talked to Kev and Tec as well; he had arrived a week before me. We got to catch up quickly, and they sent me more food and some CDs for the CD player. I didn't know how desperately I was going to need a CD player until I got to Lucasville. The block stayed loud, and the CO's allowed it. They allowed everything imaginable in this block. I was ordered to do six months in 4B, which is a step under then being in the hole. You get a few more privileges, but it's still pure torture.

The next morning, they brought us our food. I could hear the loudly squeaking food cart moving slowly toward me. It seemed like I had been waiting forever for them to reach my cell. The worker, I believe, slid a thin pink tray on my slot, which was located on the right-hand side in the middle of the bars of the door that opens. The slot was just big enough to fit the tray, which had a little bit of oatmeal, two slices of bread, and two boiled eggs. Everything on the tray was cold as fuck, and I didn't eat eggs, so I just left them on the tray. The oatmeal was too cold and disgusting-looking that I couldn't eat it, so all I ate that morning was the bread. When lunch and dinner came, it was the same thing. The food was cold, and there wasn't that much on the trays. I knew I was in for one hell of a ride being at Lucasville. I hadn't seen anything yet. I wasn't mentally prepared for the things that took place after my first week in Lucasville. I was in hell, and I had to adapt to it, which wasn't easy. There wasn't anything easy about being in Lucasville.

During my first week in Lucasville, I witnessed some of the most disgusting things I had ever seen men do. On my 3rd or 4th day there, this guy in his late 40's named Maurice Page threw a bowl of shit on someone. I couldn't believe what my eyes were seeing. My first thought was what I would do to somebody if they ever tried to throw shit on me. Then I understood how much we have to live up to and that they view black men as animals. That was the first time I thought maybe we are just that, caged animals. It was the first time I had that thought, but not the last. I saw so many crazy and inhumane things.

That old nigga, Maurice, was as crazy as they come. He had been in solitary confinement for over ten years, and his mind was fried. He thought the things he was doing were normal. He used to cell bang all day and night. He would wake everybody up at about 5 o'clock every morning with what he called roll call by beating on the bars to make a rap beat and yelling every cell number. He might say something like, *Is cell one a hater? Yea, that bitch ass dick sucking weak pussy black ass a muthafucka a hater. Kill his ass.* And then he'd go *blah, blah, blah,* making a noise with his mouth like a machine gun. Then he'd move on to the next cell and do it again, calling different names. Maurice used to play a foul game back there in 4B. We were in our cells 23 hours a day and had one hour out for rec, but we were shackled and cuffed to go to rec. For outdoor rec, we had to walk to the end of the prison and go inside a small building where they have a bunch of cages. Each cage was equipped with a dip bar, a pull-up bar, and a sit-up bench. The cage is so small you barely have any room to walk around. Outdoor rec was the same type of thing, a tiny cage with a basketball hoop inside. The basketballs usually didn't have any air inside them, and the ones that did were tiny with lumps all over them. The whole situation was fucked up. I hated being in 4B.

During those six months, I witnessed some of the craziest things I have ever seen men do to one another and themselves. The living conditions were unsanitary. The whole prison was infested with mice, and these were some of the most aggressive mice I have ever seen in my life. The mice used to come out of the vent connected to the wall on the bottom range. I used to hear them making their little squeaking noises. All through the night, you could hear them running from one end of the vent to the other. There was a hole at each end of the vent, and they would jump out. One night, I woke up because of a noise. It sounded like someone was going through the bag a food I had on the floor underneath my bunk. I leaned over, and a big ass mouse was looking me right in my face. It scared the shit out of me at first; then, I scared it out of my cell. It ran so fast I couldn't hit it with anything. After that, I couldn't sleep. I jumped up with every little sound that I heard.

    It seemed like every night after that, I was catching mice running in and out of my cell. One night, I found one on top of my cabinet, where I kept my clothes and hygiene. I didn't understand how the hell it made it all the way up on top of the cabinet. That's when I found out they can jump high as hell. After about a month, Willy and I had gotten cool; he was the porter, which means he was let out his cell to help us get things. We used to play cards. He had been sentenced to life and had been in prison for 25 years. Willy was here when the Lucasville riot took place. You wouldn't know by looking at him that he been in prison since the 80's because he kept himself up and worked out every day. He was big as fuck, built like a linebacker in the NFL. Willy gave me a lot of game on being in Lucasville, so I learned what to expect and what I needed to do to stay out of trouble. Still, I found staying out of trouble would be hard.

Samuel Woods

Chapter 11: Worst of the Worst

After being in that intake block for about five months, they moved me to another block for only four more weeks before I was released to K-6, which was the gang block. It was where the high-risk prisoners were housed. They had all the toughest, baddest muthafuckas in one block. Each block held 80 inmates, so at least 60 of them were real gang members. I knew walking into this block I had to have my eyes open, and I had to be ready to hold my own at any moment.

"Ohlllleeeee!"

I heard somebody yell my name as I was walking my bags to my cell. I could tell it was my nigga Big Kev. I knew he would be in this block. He was a gangster for sure.

"What's up, Brah? Where you at?" I yelled back.

"I'm down here, bro," he said, waving his hand out another shoot, which was a slot that you could look through and reach your hand through. The cells had doors instead of bars. I thought that was cool; I didn't want anybody to be looking all in my cell anyway.

"Oh, I see you, Brah. What's up?"

"Listen, I'm a holla at you when we go to rec, alright. You good, right?"

"Yea, I'm good. When we got rec?" I said as I set my bags down inside my cell.

"In a about an hour, so be ready, alright!" Kev said.

As he pulled his shoot back up, my cell door was closing. I looked around for a minute to take in where I was. It wasn't loud like being in the hole, which was good. I wasn't trying to hear more of that yelling back in forth what they were going to do to each other, knowing they couldn't do shit since we were locked down all day long, and we were in chains and shackles wherever we went. If you wanted to get at whoever you were beefing with, you had to go to rec and crash on the rec chain, which means head bumping, spitting on them, or if you have a small wrist, slipping the cuffs off to fuck the man up. I saw a white boy slip the cuffs and pull a shank out from his draws and stab the shit out of another white boy. The COs beat them like crazy.

In Lucasville, the COs carry billy clubs like cops. If inmates are fighting and don't stop when told, they start hitting them with those clubs until they stop. They get nasty with those sticks, especially if you're black. I felt a stick or two during my five years I spent in hell on earth.

Big Kev was from Cleveland. He was 6' 5" with a little weight on him, not that tall skinny shit, and he had work. He knew how to throw them hands for his height. He bared none, and he was like a brother to me. We had been rocking since the day I met him.

"Alright, listen, Brah. This shit sweet for real, but you got some gangstas over here. We like 12 deep. I'm a introduce you to everybody. We good. We got some hitters. It's like ten Crips, like 11 GDs, and about 20 ABs. You know this they back yard, but shit, we good. This shit. We got the ticket bro running it. You need anything, let me know, brah. Other than that, just stay on point, alright."

"Shit, you already know I'm a stay on point, no doubt."

Everything bro told me was helpful as far as just knowing who was who and what was what. After he introduced me to everybody, I knew that I had a couple of solid niggas around me. The other ones were suspect.

"Aye, Ohle, you need anything?" the homie who ran the ticket asked.

"Nah, I'm straight, my nigg. Good look, though." I replied quickly. I didn't know these niggas, so I wasn't trying to befriend anybody. I wanted to see who was who first. That whole night I was in deep thought about how and what I was about to do. I wasn't expecting to see what I saw the next day, but it made me change my outlook.

I was sitting in my cell watching TV when I heard a squeaking noise like somebody was fighting. I went to my cell door window and saw one white boy stabbing another white boy. He wasn't stopping; he was trying to kill the dude. I thought he was going to stop when the COs and white shirts came running into the block, but he didn't. He had him held with one arm wrapped around his neck while the other one was stabbing his side. You could hear him screaming. The white dude couldn't escape him. I thought that muthafucka was about to be dead. The COs just stood there trying to negotiate with him to put the knife down. When they realized he wasn't going stop, they rushed him. The guy had been stabbed over 30 times. My first thought was that I needed a shank, so as soon they let us out for lunch, I walked up on the homie who asked me if I needed something.

"Aye, you asked me if I needed something. Well, yea, man, I do. I need a shank ASAP."

"You for real?" he asked.

"Yea, I'm dead serious, brah."

"I got you."

The next morning, I had a shank in my possession. It didn't take long at all. I just wanted to be safe. I didn't know what was going on in this block. They said it was the worst of the worst gang members in the prison system, so I wasn't taking any chances period. I felt more comfortable once I had that shank. I never had to use it, but it was nice to know I had one in case I needed it.

After watching one of the worst stabbings since I had been in prison, I was on high alert. There were some fucked up individuals in there who didn't give a fuck about anything, including their lives. I watched an inmate fight with the COs. I've seen a prisoner take a CO's billy club and beat him with it. He chased him around, hitting him with the stick until other COs came in and saved their co-worker. The longer I was in Lucasville, the better I understood why they called it the worst prison in Ohio. After a few months in K-6, I saw about four stabbings and a bunch of fights, but I couldn't believe how guys were getting raped. It was crazy.

I saw a couple of white boys get raped. I didn't see them actually getting raped, but this old school guy was known for that. They called him a booty bandit, which means he tries to fuck every young white boy he can. I saw him slide into a couple of these white boys' cells. They screamed, but he would make them shut up, and he would do them. Then you would see the white boy with a black eye the next day. The other thing was, I never seen so many niggas who pulled their dicks out and told another man to suck their dicks. That was going on all over Lucasville. You would think that nigga would get killed, but some would fight, and others would be scared of the nigga who pulled out on him and would use every excuse not to do anything. I couldn't wait to get the fuck away from this type of shit.

I had a job working in the 4B blocks as a porter. That is where I would make my money. If you didn't have family or friends who were sending cash, you needed a hustle like running a store. For example, you might give somebody a bag of chips until we went back to the store for two bags back. Or you might run a ticket for football or basketball depending on the season. You could also be into extortion. You only could shop twice a month so by the time you went back to the store, all your food would be gone. You could hustle some money up working in 4B. You could get paid real money for bringing someone food items they couldn't have back there.

Also, back then, tobacco was still being sold in the prisons. I would buy two cans of burglar tobacco, and I would sell the cans for $75. I would have other inmates pick up more cans for me, so I could have more to sell. I was selling tobacco and my nigga's pills. He was taking Tramadol, which was a medication that got you high. They went for $2 each. My nigga was diabetic, so he would get nine pills throughout the day. I worked every other day, so he would have 18 pills for me when I came back to work. I would save those until I reached 100 and sell them all for money on the streets. I was running scams, all types of shit to get that paper. I was 23 with $1,500 on my books from the hustle. I moved differently than the average 23-year-old. You wouldn't know I was 23 until I told you. Most people thought I was older because of the way I moved and carried myself. Being in Lucasville made me grow up faster. I learned how to manage money and look at situations from a different perspective than I did when I first came to prison. I was being molded. I worked out six times a week by myself, but I was trying to better myself physically and mentally. I still was trapped in the belly of the beast, and I still had anger issues.

I always seemed to have self-destructive tendencies. It was like I couldn't get it together for anything. My anger was the reason for almost all the things I put myself through. I had a short temper, which led to me being in a maximum prison. Most people think prisons are designed to rehabilitate you. However, there are few programs available to help you become a better citizen. They have these little childish programs like "Cage our Rage," in which they ask you some of the dumbest questions. They don't have any solutions at the end of the packet they give you. They want to keep the program running for financial reasons. It's all about money in prison. They couldn't care less about if you change or not. They want you to come back so they can get that money the taxpayers pay on your behalf. I have done all the programs they had to offer, and none of them worked because they weren't hands-on with the program. All the case managers did was hand you a packet for the program and tell you to answer the questions and give it back. There aren't any classes, and there's no one to hear you tell your story so they can give advice. It's all about the completions so the prison can turn it in and make it seem like they are running their programs properly, but that isn't the case. It's also why my anger issues never subsided. I just got worse as the years passed.

After about seven months in population, I got into a little group fight with some GDs that had got into it with my nigga Lambo. We had each other's backs since we were 15 years old in juvie, so when he fought, I fought with him, which landed us back in the hole. I stayed in the hole for 18 months straight. I saw the nastiest craziest weirdest things one could ever imagine. It was the first time I saw shit turn into maggots due to the shit sitting for so long. Some inmates held bottles filled with shit, and If you got into an argument with them, they would throw shit on you. That was their way of fighting you. We would call spitting on someone or throwing bottles of shit and pee on someone a cowardly act, but this is what was going on in 4B. It was another world, even for prison. Two dudes hung themselves because they couldn't take it anymore. I've seen COs beat inmates so severely that they broke their ribs and split their heads open. They don't talk about these things, but it is happening.

When I was released after those 18 months in the hole, it felt like I was going home. I was so happy to get out of that hell hole. You would think that a person would do everything possible to get out of 4B, but you had guys who went back there because they couldn't manage on the compound. They probably didn't have a TV of their own, which is a big must since you're locked down all day every day.

I was sent to the other side of the prison, which was L-side. I was in L- 3. The blocks are the same with 80 inmates in it, but there were straight bars, no doors, or slots that you can stick your arms through. It was different from 4B, and there was a different caliber of inmates. I didn't get to stay in L-3 for long because I had beef with a couple of cats. The first person was this nigga named Cash. He was doing 14 years for killing my son's mother's cousin in a car accident. He had been driving drunk and killed all three people in the wreck. Everybody died except him, so ever since I got to prison, I had been trying to beat his ass. Jasmine was my son's mother's aunt, who had been a big part of my life since I was 16, and she had been there for me while I was doing those ten years. I was not even out of the hole for 24 hours before I was back in there for fighting.

    I had caught Cash coming to chow when I was coming back. I beat his ass quickly; it was a flawless victory. The nigga didn't even get a punch off. The sucker slammed the shit out of me, though, which made me mad as hell. I blanked out and just flipped, got on top of him and started beating his ass out until the COs came. One approached from behind me and pulled me off him by placing one of those billy clubs under my neck and lifted me high off my feet into the air and spraying me with mace. There was so much mace on my face that it was dripping off my chin. They then quickly put me in handcuffs and rushed me to the hole.

    As I was being handcuffed, I could hear the nigga say, "He crossed the line on me. He crossed on me!" Telling and shit. He later took out, though, when it was time to go in front of the board. It's like court; they bring you before three people, one might be a case manager, and the others may be sergeants, for you to try to plead your case. They determine whether you are truthful as to whatever it is you are facing as far as whatever rule you may have broken, or they said you broke. Most of the time, they find you guilty.

    It's not often they let people go with a not guilty. I mean, there must be absolutely no evidence that links you, or you are getting that guilty verdict for sure. Even though he admitted to crossing the line on me, I still had to do six more months in 4B. This time I wasn't getting into trouble; I stayed out the way so I could get back to the compound. By this time, I only had about 18 months left on my ten-year sentence. I started writing my book during those six months I had to do in 4B. If I was going to stay out of trouble, I needed to find something constructive to do, or I wouldn't keep my nose clean. So, I started writing. I always had a drive for writing. I mean, I wrote rap songs and was good at telling stories, painting pictures, and saying what's going on around me, but this was a challenge for me, and I was willing to take it on. I have read many books over the years, and some weren't that good. I used to think to myself, *I know I could have written a better book than that*. It was a lack of patience, I think, that made me not want to write. I would think *Damn, it's gonna take me forever to write a book and all the proper spelling and punctuation.* Many different things used to block my ability to move forward. Still, after all the fears went out the window, I started writing what would become a trilogy.

I finished my first book after about 12 months. Then the second book was part two, which I finished in eight months. I tried to make them different from the typical urban books that I had read. I loved the True to the Game and Dutch trilogies by Teri Woods. Those were good hood books, but I wanted to mix my books up. I didn't want them to be the same average books with the same concepts. So, I made my book about a two-pound red ruby everyone was fighting over.

Unfortunately, I couldn't finish the trilogy. Parts one and two were thrown away by an ex's family member. That was devastating. It left me with heartache; those books were like my babies. I liked the feeling I had after finishing those books. It was the best feeling in the world to have something I could cherish and live on after I'm gone; something I can say I did that was positive. Knowing I accomplished something like that while I was in prison, one of the roughest prisons in Ohio at that, was significant. So, for somebody to destroy my manuscripts was deeply hurtful. I dreaded anything like that happening again.

You're probably wondering how that happened. I was irresponsible. It happened when I caught my third number, so I wasn't present to protect my books. It's a lesson that I learned for so many different reasons. After doing ten years, it's a must for one to have accomplished e something constructive, something positive to show for all those years spent in prison. *I mean, what have you done to show that you have become a changed person?* This is a fundamental question that one must ask and give an honest answer.

I never thought I would write books, but I did. That is how I came to believe the saying that anything you put your mind to you can do. I'm living proof of that right now, but I wasn't ready mentally. My heart wasn't right yet. I came home after ten years of imprisonment and didn't do anything. I didn't do shit to help my family and me. I didn't get those books published, which was the dumbest thing I could have ever done, but at that time, my mind was not right. Even after ten years locked up, my way of thinking hadn't changed. It was like I had gotten worse, but the only question is, *how is that?* Why didn't I grow for the better, but instead, the worse? Here is the question we all want to be answered. Why do so many people come out of prison without having changed or even wanting to change? Why is this a common problem in America today?

Part 2: System, Cycle, & Broken Aspirations

Chapter 12: Systematic Struggle

Why is it one out of three black men released from prison return to prison within the first 90 to 180 days after being home? That hasn't been figured out yet. To this day, the cycle is in full effect.

I'm living proof of that fact. After doing ten years in prison, I was on my way back for gun and drug charges after being home for only four months. You may wonder how I got myself into a situation where I could be accused of basically the same crimes I have been being charged with since I was a teenager. I'm going to explain why I, and so many others, fall victim to the cycle of recidivism.

The pattern had to start somewhere, right? To understand the situation, we must ask where the problem lies. It is easy to say we are the problem, but let's be logical. We are living in a broken system. The system is supposed to help change the way we live and think. It is made to keep the social order, yet the court system doesn't follow its own laws. Instead, they bend the rules to suit their goals and try to sweep the truth under the rug. The courts are full of corruption, and they will do anything to hide their deceit. It is more common than you can imagine for the attorneys and judges to break the law themselves to get a conviction.

Black males have been caught in this cycle, which leads to us into this broken system in which is not successful at rehabilitation. Prisons were built by rich white men to control the economy to control other men and women. Without punishment, men and women would be able to do what they wanted, even if it caused harm. Prisons were built to ensure there would be consequences for breaking any laws.

If you are caught breaking the law, you go to jail. It is as simple as that. There are alternatives, like being put on probation. This is called getting cut a break. When you're sentenced to probation, the court sets whatever time you were initially facing on the shelf. If you violate the terms of your probation, you can be sent to jail to serve the time that was set aside. The court gives you just enough rope to hang yourself because it's much easier to break the terms of most probation agreements than to keep them.

That applies to everything dealing with the system. The court system is where it starts. You have to go through the court system before you reach the prison system, and the government runs both. You may come across some privately-owned prisons, but the government has its dirty paws all over it.

Before I was even born, the court system was handing down outrageous sentences. In the '70s and '80s, the laws were very different from today. Back then, they would give you a sentence with a tail, which meant, for example, you would have to serve eight to 15 years in prison with 15 being the tail and eight being the initial time you would have to do. After serving the initial sentence of eight years, you would be eligible to get an earlier release, also known as parole. If you have a good behavior report, then you would be released. If not, you would be most likely looking at serving the additional seven years.

How can you fix somebody who is already broken in more ways than you could ever imagine? Prison is designed to break you, and it has broken so many. After doing so much time in prison, it begins to tear you apart mentally and physically. It destroys all hope. Often, prisoners find themselves wondering what they have to live for; they've often lost key relationships with spouses and children. Parents and grandparents may have passed away. When you feel you have no reason to live, you don't see a reason to change. Why try to become a better person and a better citizen if you feel as if you are worthless?

This is what is happening, and nobody has a solution for it. You might be thinking, *Well, it's their own fault. Everybody has the same opportunities. They had a choice, but they chose to commit crimes and break the laws.* There may be some truth to those statements, but how can we change the cycle? Why hasn't anything meant to help lead us down another path made significant changes? There are a variety of reasons our communities are broken. However, gangs and drugs taking over entire communities is probably the biggest problem, and I was part of that problem in my community. It is time for a change. If we utilize every tool at our disposal, the change will come.

Change may occur when the court system changes. That's what's wrong. That's where the real problem lies, not with us, but with the ones who have a state prison number on their resume. It's the judges with no mercy for a human being. They are the real problem that has the system so fucked up.

Where do I start? Let me start by saying the court system is set up to keep you stuck inside their web of corruption. The judges, prosecutors, and lawyers are all working together. I'm going to tell how they treat us. I can't speak about any other place, but I'm quite sure Canton, Ohio, isn't any different than any other state. People are getting railroaded all over America.

The court system I've been dealing with since I was 18, plays the game raw. They over-indict you so they can force you to take a plea deal so they can avoid paying for a trial. Trials cost money, so they try everything in their power to make you take a plea. Through the course of going through the court system, you will deal with the shadiness of grimy lawyers. We call them "deal lawyers" because their job is to get you to take a deal and save the court money. Now you have an over-charged indictment, meaning they then put extra and unnecessary charges on there. And, you get a court-appointed lawyer due to the fact you can't afford a paid lawyer, so your lawyer isn't even working for you from the jump. The courts are paying him to represent you. They tell you if you can't afford an attorney, then one will be provided for you. What they don't tell you is that the attorney will be working for the state, so their job will be to make sure they send you to prison and get that $47,000 the taxpayers pay to finance your stay.

While you are going through the process, the lawyer will give you all the reasons why you won't win at trial if you decide to go. He will say that if you lose at trial, you will be facing 30 years after all those trumped-up charges. Then he will say they have all kinds of evidence against you, all to make you scared and to force you to take the deal that the judge has offered you. The lawyer won't care if you are innocent or not. "Innocent until proven guilty" doesn't exist in the real world; you have to work hard to prove your innocence nowadays. Until then, you will be treated as if you did the crime. Everyone from the judges to the prosecutor is going to play it like you did whatever you were accused of. Even if you do have a paid lawyer, evidence that could exonerate you will be hidden from you. The prosecution will withdraw relevant evidence so you will be unable to prepare a proper defense. That is where the corruption comes into play. This is what I mean when I say, "they call us losers, yet they have to cheat to win." Even the cops will lie and plant evidence on you. The police are just as dirty. I swear, in Canton, nobody is honest, and nobody follows the law. I mean nobody.

So now you have been sentenced, but the laws have changed now: instead of receiving a tail sentence, they are giving out flat time. Meaning if you receive ten years, then you must do ten years to the day. They may say that you can be up for an early release after 85% of your time has been served. Even then, only the judge has the power to release you, and I haven't seen one person from Canton, Ohio, get out after serving 85% of their time if you have a violent charge. Now, they give those people with drug charges a slap on the wrist. You saw it: Obama released over 20 inmates with a drug offense. How many did he release with a shooting case or a robbery charge? Not one, so what does that show you? It shows you that the government helps bring the drugs into the cities, and they look out for their own kind. They want the drug dealers to be free, so they can keep selling the drugs to the addicts, the ones that keep robbing and stealing and killing for their next high. This prevents the crime rate from declining.

Now let's dig a little deeper into this court system and how it's being run. The sole purpose of the judge handing out these outrageous sentences is to keep us on our backs. You have black men doing 15 years for robbery, but they have no programs or rehabs for that. Where are the rehabs for the guy who got three to four robberies and thefts on his record? See, they forget about them, yet they have all types of rehabs and programs for the drug users. Let me explain to you why. Blacks and whites use drugs at about the same rate, but the imprisonment rate of blacks for drug charges is almost six times that of whites. You have these affluent white kids strung out on drugs, so they build these facilities to try to help them but forget about the ones who need help to quit stealing, which is an addiction too. Now, they have heroin taking over the world, and wealthy white families are suffering from their child being strung out on the drug or overdosing.

Now they are trying to change the law. They are trying to change how you can get prescription pills. Everything is about the money and the protection of rich white people. What about us? What about those who live in the ghetto, smack in the middle of all the drugs, gangs, and violence? What about the ones who are face to face with these horrible things every single day? They "forget" about us. They forget about us on purpose. They want us to kill and rob each other; sell each other drugs that have been destroying our communities for decades. That is where they make their money. They can use all those shady tactics to keep us buried in the system. They know that the upper class isn't committing any crimes like the ones that you have in the black or minority communities. They have a whole different set of rules. They do white-collar crimes like racketeering. Also, a lot of them like messing with minors. We have seen them get probation for having sex with a minor but then receive three to seven years for racketeering. The laws change when it comes to the rich. They don't get treated the same. Neither do the police.

The police are the biggest gang I have ever seen. They continuously get away with breaking the law. Cops catch DUI's, and nothing happens to them, but if we catch a DUI, our licenses get suspended, or we spend time in the county jail. You see cops killing people all the time. You see them do it with no remorse or anything, killing unarmed young black men. They get no punishment for their crimes; how can you explain that? There's no justification for a police officer shooting an unarmed black man in the streets and not getting charged with murder. Some don't even lose their job. According to the Department of Justice, one in three black men can expect to go to prison in their lifetime. Individuals of color have a disproportionate number of encounters with law enforcement, indicating that racial profiling continues to be a huge problem. Another report by the Department of Justice found that blacks and Hispanics were approximately three times more likely to be searched during a traffic stop than whites. Blacks are twice as likely to be arrested and four times as likely to experience the use of force during encounters with the police, as you can see with all these killings of black men and women by police officers.

It's a shame that this is the type of example the law enforcement set for the community. On the news, I once saw a cop jump on top of a car and shoot multiple bullets into a suspect's windshield in Cleveland, Ohio. Altogether, there were over 200 bullets fired into the victim's car, which killed him and the passenger. All the cops that were involved were later acquitted. That is an injustice of the most unimaginable kind. There are Mike Browns and Trayvon Martins all over the country who, to this day, haven't received any justice. Why can cops break the law? They violate the same rules they are supposed to enforce and don't face any consequences. That is the definition of a broken system, and not just me, but millions are trapped in it. They make sure we can never escape the claws of the system by giving us mandatory years of parole after we serve years in prison.

    I had been released from a ten-year sentence after giving the judge every single day. When I came home, and I was on five-year mandatory parole. How could that be? It is cruel and unusual punishment. They make sure they give you multiple years of probation. That way, if you stay clean for the first two years, maybe the last one you mess up, and they can send you back to prison. It's a dirty game. Why, after serving a full sentence, would you still have to serve a second sentence? Parole involves multiple years of control over what you can do, where you can live, when to be in the house, and who to have as your friends. It's double punishment, but it's all about keeping the cycle going so they can keep jails and prisons packed. They maintain that flow of inmates coming through. For every 37 adults in the United States, 27% is under some form of adult supervision.

Chapter 13: Revolving Doors to a Crippled Society

The cycle is a never-ending revolving door that will never be shut, and we are stuck in it. It's hard to break free from the grasp of the system when judges hand out long sentences and unfair mandatory paroles in which the parole officers' objective is to send you back as opposed to trying to help you stay home. That is why it is so hard for us, the less fortunate, to become productive citizens. We don't have financial stability. We come out of prison to a society that won't give us a job because we have a criminal record. The negative impact of a criminal record is twice as significant for black job applicants. Still, your PO tries to give you a deadline to get a job, or he will violate you. It's not an easy task for felons. Yet, we get shit on. We probably never had an honest job in our lives, and now we're forced to get one with no skills or trades. It's why a lot of us go back to selling drugs and robbing because then we have to do something to help their families.

It's hard to change someone who is stuck in their ways. How do you change a man who has been the same way for over 20 or 30 years? It's hard to reach them to help them become better men and better citizens. That's why we need to catch the youth before they develop habits that are hard to shake. This book is meant to shed light on the system and how it affects us as a whole. The government needs to create programs for new releases that will help them learn trades so they can get jobs. Instead, they want to make weed legal so they can make some money rather than help the crime rate go down and turn known addicts or drug dealers into a productive citizen. It is crazy how the world is. I'm living in this broken system that's structured to keep us held back and keep us stuck in the never-ending cycle. The only way we can break the cycle is if we do it ourselves. We must find our own solution. We must work together as a community to break the cycle. When I was coming up, there were no programs that we kids could go to, no boxing gyms, no centers that would help teach us anything constructive, and no positive role models. As I think about it now, how did they ever think we were going to turn out to be some good kids when bills needed to be paid, and we lived in crack houses in neighborhoods full of gang members? What route do you think one is going to take when all he is around is gangs, drugs, and violence? We have to be real with ourselves, which is why we need to start putting positive things the youth can look up to in the communities and save some of the kids. We're not going to save every kid on the block, but we can save some, and some are better than none.

I've touched on the system, and how it's run to destroy us. Yet, the politicians try to call prisons the facilities of rehabilitation, but who are they rehabilitating? Only one out of every ten or 15 releases turn their lives around and become productive in society. How can you expect one to adapt to a community that he has been away from for 20 years? After being locked down for 20 years, not being able to go through the experiences of a free man, please explain to me how one can come home and adapt to the life of a free man. How can one be expected to work a regular job and be able to talk and socialize around people when all he knows is the life of an inmate? We need re-adjustment programs to help those who have done many years inside a prison wall learn how to function in the real world. Maybe, this will help to reduce the same results of us coming back to prison after being released from prison. This is what needs to be done, but you don't see the government doing any of these things because they want us to fail. They don't want us to excel or rise above their expectations. They want to keep their feet on our backs so we can't elevate ourselves

What are we going to do to bring change to the cycle of young black men cycling through prisons? How are we going to fix this problem? The real question is: what are you going to do? What's needed from you to make that transition? It's going to take a lot of will power, a lot of strength, and a lot of readjustments.

It is hard to change, to become a better person, to escape the things we have been living with for most of our life. Nobody is going to hold your hands in this world of sin. You must be willing to make a difference in your own life. You have to put yourself in a position to make your situation better. Positioning is everything. I

Imprisonment

used to hear actors and music artists say they were at the right place at the right time when they caught their break. Changing your life is the same thing. You want to put yourself in a better position so that you can have opportunities to make your life better. It's not that hard. We choose not to take the initiative to want to take the steps that are needed to make that change.

For example, why do you go back to the same hood and hang around the same people who probably are doing the same things they were doing before you went to prison? How do you expect to find a better way of living when you went right back to the same environment knowing the same results are waiting for you? Why don't we ever change locations and friends? Different decisions and ways of living will bring different results. Yet, we still refuse to take a chance on taking a different approach. I'm tired of hearing that same old line, "shit, this is all I know." I used to use that same line, and it's our excuse for being a repeated felon. People try and justify their reasons by saying all they know how to do is sell dope, rob, steal, or even kill. Is this true?

Many will say yes because they train their minds to think like that or because they never experience anything other than running the streets. That may be so, but what do we do now, what steps do we or can we take to end the cycle we accustomed to?

It's not just dealing with the streets once you are released because, in reality, the change must start before release from prison. That is where the problem lies. We tend to allow the ways of the outside world to defeat us. We fall for the system's tricks and lose sight of becoming better people. We tend to get caught up in the prison life where we get high and try to find ways to get drugs we can sell to make money. We get involved in gangs even more than we did on the streets because, these days, gangs run the prisons. We figure out ways to become better criminals rather than how to be better fathers to our kids or better sons to our parents. It's essential to start the transformation while still incarcerated, so when we get out, we will be mentally ready to move forward.

I know this from experience. When it was time for me to come home, I wasn't ready. Although I told myself I was ready, I wasn't even close. I still was getting into fights and all that type of nonsense. Neither my mind nor my heart was ready. Within 12 days after my release, I got locked up again. My parole officer (P.O.) violated my parole due to me being a suspect in a murder investigation. I was sent to the county jail after I turned myself in.

Of course, I was innocent. After they did their investigation, they found out my alibi was solid, and there wasn't enough evidence to charge me. I was finally released from jail but was dropped off at a rehabilitation house in Akron, Ohio, where I wasn't supposed to be in the first place. After the house was approved, I was released from the rehabilitation house. I knew I wasn't supposed to be there because they didn't even have me in their computer.

Basically, they tried to hold me for more time in hopes they would find something on me. After I got out, I was living in Columbus. The first couple of months were cool, but I still was driving to Canton. It was like I couldn't stay away. I knew I should have stayed out of the way in Columbus, but no, I just had to be in Canton. Although I had to see my P. O. twice a month, I still made my way down to Canton. The next thing I knew, I was back in jail facing drug and gun charges. The cops busted into a bar and found three pistols and about 28 grams of crack cocaine. The drugs were found in the bar, but not on any person. I was charged and was the only one whose charges stuck. Everybody else who was in the bar got out on a no bill. I got nine months in prison. After receiving those nine months, you would think I would sit down and leave the streets alone, but while I was in prison, I was looking to still carry guns and sell drugs. I know it doesn't make any sense. What does it take for someone to say enough is enough?

When we are in prison, most of us tend to try to learn how not to get caught the next time. Instead of planning for a good future, we often plan for destruction. Nine times out of ten, as soon as we get released and return back to the old neighborhood and old friends, we end up facing new charges. It's just that simple. The only way we're going to break this horrible cycle is by having something with which we can help our own. Let's build a solid foundation to help break the cycle.

After being released from prison the second time, I was still heading in the wrong direction. I didn't know what I wanted out of life, so it wasn't long before I was on my third number. Living what we call the street life, only two things are going to happen. You either are going to be killed, or you will go to prison for years, possibly even life. When you are living the street life, you only have two options, death or imprisonment. There is no other way out except to get out of the life. You must be serious about what you want and if it is to leave the street life then you know that's what you have to do. Many want to get out of the life, but they do not

Imprisonment

know how to make that transition. We need to find a solution to the problem of recidivism.

We first have to drop the percentage on recidivism by setting up programs for new releases to give us work coming straight out of prison. We need to be able to provide parolees jobs so that they can have income. One of the main reasons a lot of felons get released and find themselves back on the streets selling drugs is because they have no income coming in to take care of their families and themselves. Once released, the reality of being free and faced with responsibilities hits fast. Most can't cope with not being able to make money, so they commit robberies or sell drugs, which leads to them getting locked back up again.

To avoid that cycle, we must have a program set up for those getting released that will give them the help that's needed to get them on the right path. The government receives thousands of dollars for each person who gets sent to prison. Yet, the Governor doesn't invest that money into programs that give the recently released a fighting chance to become productive citizens in their communities. Some inmates are coming off 20- or 30-year sentences, and they have lost their whole families. They have no one to turn to and no place to live when they get out of prison. Programs to help former felons access jobs and affordable housing are needed to help keep the recidivism down.

We can stop the recidivism by giving the up and coming kids in our community something more to look forward to in life. The government could build recreational centers instead of building prisons in poor communities. We need a program that will teach kids how to be more productive citizens by doing something other than drug sales and learning how to kick a door in. We will cut the percentage in half of the never-ending cycle of blacks going back and forth to prison with a program like this. Change isn't easy, but if you have a good system to teach kids how to do better and execute meaningful life lessons, then we will be getting somewhere. I think if you show that the end results are rewarding, then more kids will fall into the line of righteous living.

When you want something in life, but you must work to obtain it, you sometimes get discouraged, right? I remember when I came home from doing those ten years in prison. My kids wanted this and wanted that and everything. I bought them so many things because I felt like I owed them the world.

My older sister, Ebony, used to tell me all the time to quit buying the kids all that stuff. She told me I was spending too much money on the kids. She got mad when I spent $1,500 on shoes and clothes when I was fresh out of prison. I had been home only a couple of days, and she let me have it, "Boy, you tripping! I could of went to a cheap store and got them a shit load of clothes and shoes for that type of money." I didn't realize it at the time, but I wasn't giving them anything to work toward or for.

After my sister and I had that conversation, I told my kids that to receive anything from me, they needed to bring me good grades on their report cards. The first time my kids brought me all A's and B's, I went out and bought them expensive cell phones. That was all the motivation they needed. They started to ask me for things, and I would tell them if you want that new pair of shoes, you know what that report card better say. They made sure they brought me A's and B's.

The kids started getting good grades, and they couldn't wait to tell me. Because they knew if they had good grades, they had something nice coming from Dad. Through the course of it all, I made sure I taught them the importance of education. They loved me for that, and I felt good knowing that my kids went out to learn and do well in school. People tend to work harder when they are working hard for something they want.

The same thing happens with guys in prison. When the judge says if you can stay ticket free and not go to the hole (segregation), I will give you a judicial, which is an early release. A minority will do just that so that they can be released early. They do what they must do to get what they want. Why can't it be as easy for guys coming home from prison? It's because they have nothing to work for, so why don't we start giving these guys something to work toward, something they can and will put the work in to obtain, whatever it is they need to make it through? For example, let's say you just got released, and you don't have anywhere to live. The government could enroll you in a job-training program with job placement upon completion.

There isn't any program in place right now like this, but I believe this would work. I'm just saying these are solutions. We need to explore these platforms to seek change in this judicial system. If we want to see a shift in society, we need to minimize crime. We can do this by encouraging businesses to give the less fortunate jobs, so they have better options than the streets. Each one of you can positively affect society. If each person would teach one person, we can reach one soul after another until we start up an epidemic. When a new drug hits our streets, it spreads like wildfire. We can use that word of mouth for good. If we hit our streets and feed people with righteousness, such as righteous ways of living and how to give back, we can positively affect society.

Samuel Woods

Part 3: Growth & Development

Samuel Woods

Imprisonment

Chapter 14: A Mind Is a Powerful Thing to Waste

What is something that is not growing? Something that is not growing is dead. For that matter, a lot of us are running around dead. Many of us are lost and have no clue what life is about or what we want out of life. The question is, what is it you want out of your life?

Education is probably the most crucial thing one must gain during his or her lifetime. Still, a lot of us tend not to take it seriously. I stopped going to school at the age of 16. I believe I was heading to the 10th grade. I never made it, which is sad and doesn't make sense. Yet, at the time, I thought school was holding me back. You may wonder *what was more important than getting an education?*

I thought running the streets, selling drugs, and kicking it with my boys was more important. I thought I was supposed to be messing with different women. I was fooled, and I was stupid as hell. When I look at all those silly decisions I made as a teen, I regret it all. I was misinformed as a youth about how I was supposed to live my life. It wasn't until I caught a life sentence that I started to look at life differently. I wasn't living the dream I thought I was. I was living the nightmare. I won't go into a lot of details about things I was doing because I don't want to glorify that life. We tend to glorify the street life like that's the American dream, driving in beautiful cars, living in nice houses, and messing with pretty women. You know, the life we glorify like that's the right way to live, but it's not. All that shit goes out the window as soon as you lose it.

I was taking my life for granted for all those years. It took the judge handing me 35 years to life on my third number for me to start looking at my life differently and seeing that the way I was living wasn't working. I didn't begin to change my way of thinking right away. It was years before I made the transition of working on myself for the better. It started with my thought patterns. I knew after I conquered my way of thinking, I could dig into my every being as a man, who I was, and to who I wanted to become if I put my mind to it.

A mind is a terrible thing to waste. I know we all have heard this saying a time or two in our lives. It is a profound quote and a true statement. If you don't educate yourself, then you are wasting your opportunity to become the next movie producer or CEO. There are so many things we can be if we put our minds to the task.

Most people tend to want things handed to them. They don't want to work for the things they want out of life, which is crazy because I was raised with the mantra that if you don't work, you don't eat. Back when I did attend school, I remember a teacher asking me what I wanted to be when I grew up. My response was an NBA basketball player. Was that dream out of reach? It was a common answer. There are a lot of kids who want to become the next Lebron, yet they rarely do. Then you have some who do go on to play in the NBA who had that dream as well. If you want to become something or be somebody, you must work hard at it, and that hard work starts with your education. I wish I would have taken school more seriously. If I had, maybe my life would have had a different outcome. It may have saved me years of incarceration. Instead, I tried to take the easy route. People often ask me why my brothers and sisters all graduated and are now living good lives. My mom often asks, "Where did I go wrong with you? How come you didn't turn out like your sisters and brothers?" I used to tell her that it wasn't anything she didn't or did do. I just made the wrong decisions. I was an angry kid. The struggle was real for us, but there was a lot of hatred in my heart for some reason. Maybe it came from the loss of my father and my stepfather. I didn't have the positive guidance I needed from the male figures in my life.

I didn't take life as seriously as I should have, which lead me to go through many pitfalls. I was heading nowhere fast and ended up in prison at the age of 18. I was still a teenager; I lost my youth to the streets and prison. I had been stripped of my childhood due to poverty. But being placed inside a prison at 18 years old with a ten-year sentence for a crime that doesn't even fit the time left me broken in every way possible. I didn't learn shit from the prison programs during those ten years. What I learned, I had to teach myself. They offer you schooling, but they limit your education in prison. For instance, if you are doing a life sentence, you can't enroll in college. You have to have five years or less to attend college. That's not a reasonable policy. Because even though you may be serving a life sentence, you still may be eligible for parole. You need the right education to get certain types of jobs and a college degree to get even better-paying jobs. Then they wonder why most people who get released from prison go back to selling drugs. They control everything inside the prison, including whether or not you get an education, knowing you need that to live a productive life once released.

There is a myth that prison is designed to help you become a better person, so once you are back on the streets, you can be more productive. Yet they don't give you many options to become a better person in prison. They say inmates 21 years of age or younger must attend school. Younger people usually are put at the top of the school list, which means inmates older than 21 have to wait to get their GEDs. That doesn't make any sense to me, given the claim that prisons are trying to rehabilitate inmates. What if that 22-year-old only has an 18-month sentence and is trying to get his GED before he is released so he can have something that will help him get a job? He can't because the waiting list is too long. Then, he gets released and says fuck school and go back to selling dope.

The government doesn't care about rehabilitation like they try to pretend. They care more about building prisons and making sure their prison system remains full as opposed to making sure schools are being built.

In 2012, the U.S. spent $81 billion on corrections. Spending on prisons and jails increased at triple the rate of spending on pre-K through 12 public education in the last 30 years, which shows me how unfortunate we are as U.S. citizens, whether we have been to prison or not. When I was released from prison, both times, I enrolled in college. I was attending Columbus State. I had taken my tests and applied for my financial aid; I just never made it to a class. I got arrested each time right before I was about to start my college classes. I'm still mad at myself for missing out on those opportunities. I always thought if I would have started college, I may have had a better outcome in my life. Who knows? I do know it took me receiving a life sentence before I realized how important my life was and how I wanted to start living it.

It's never too late to change and to become a better person. A lot of people who have life sentences tend to give up; they think it's over, and they don't try anymore. They let the system win. I'm here to tell you that you don't have to. You don't have to be just another number. You can be in prison and still be productive, maybe not to your community, but you can help others and teach young people how not to make the same mistakes you made. It is never too late, although most of us give up and say, *Fuck it! What do I have to live for?* Then we stop, but that is cowardly. If there is one thing I've learned during this process, it is that life is what you make it. Some of us made our lives hard; others made their lives easy and rewarding. How are you going to create your life?

Chapter 15: Ambitious Mind

I had made my life hard with all the bad decisions I made, but I couldn't dwell on the past. They gave me life, but that didn't mean I had to walk around like I was dead. In fact, I'm more alive now than I have ever been in my entire life, and that comes from all the positive progress I have made and still am making.

I still was getting into gang fights, getting caught with drugs, going to level four prisons, and sitting in the hole for months at a time as I fought for my freedom back. I knew I had to start changing my way of thinking first before I could even consider myself as a better person. Everything we do begins with a thought. We all know right from wrong, and if we thought before we made those bad decisions, we wouldn't have ended up in prison. So, I knew for me to become a better person, it would have to start with how my thought process was. I had to change my way of thinking to help others. I would have to get myself together on all levels, meaning I would have to stop with all the bullshit and focus on trying to give people hope. So, I read books, studied, and I built up my mind. I had all kinds of tests, and I'm not going to lie. I failed numerous times. Changing from someone you have been your whole life to become a more responsible, productive, serious, and positive person takes will power and mental strength. That's what I used.

I used my knowledge of where I was and where I felt I needed to be, and that was a free man. I put myself in a position to excel and elevate. That is how I began this journey to give all these young guys who come into prison reasons not to go back. I feel like they listen to me when I talk to them. They know I am right about most of the things I tell them, but how can I make an impact on someone's life when I am standing right next to them. They hear me, but my message won't register with them because I'm still one of them. I haven't shown them that I turned my life around by using and doing all the things I'm telling them to do because I'm still right here in prison. That is a challenge for me, yet I don't let it discourage me. None of the guys I've witnessed get released had a plan for when they got home. And I've told so many how important it is to leave with a plan. Without a plan, you are destined for disaster.

Each time I was released from prison, I did not have a plan. That's why I was a repeat felon. It is sad, but it is one of the most significant issues we have with those who are getting released from prison. They have no sense of direction. They know not where they are headed and soon return to prison. If you are incarcerated right now, you need to ask yourself what your plan is. What are you going to do after you are released from the worst place on earth? If you don't know, then right now is the time for you to answer that critical question.

I have learned that stability is one of the key factors motivating someone not to go back to breaking the law. Being stable means you have a structure you can build on and turn your life into something productive instead of turning back to the streets because you don't know where your next dollar is coming from. I noticed most guys who went home to a nice girl and a beautiful place to live had a better chance of doing better than those who go back to nothing and nobody. Stability is vital, along with having a plan. You must know what you are about to do, not just talk about it. I've seen so many guys say they were going to get a job, go to college, and as soon they get released, they are back in the streets and end up back in prison not long after that. So, one must come to the term of really taking life seriously because I know no one gets out intending to go back to prison.

While you are incarcerated and waiting to be released, you must take the time to prepare yourself for the real world. It starts with you because nobody is going to do anything for you, especially in prison. No program can prepare you for the real world. You must get your heart and soul right.

Looking at my life now after all those years of self-destruction, I've learned that the reason I kept doing the same thing is that I felt my life had no meaning. Even though I had two children who looked for me to love them and show them the way, I was lost. How could I give anybody love when I didn't love myself? It's easy to say you love yourself, but in my situation, I asked myself that question, and I use to think I did. In all honesty, I didn't give a fuck about myself or the people in my life. How could I say I loved myself and my kids when I kept putting myself in harm's way when I kept putting myself inside a prison cell? How could I say I loved myself when I consumed alcohol and smoked weed daily in front of my kids with no regard for how it's affecting them? How could I say I loved myself when I drove around with drugs on me to sell and just being up to no good? I did not love myself, and it wasn't until my life was taken away, I realized that. It wasn't until I grew as a man that I figured out the purpose of my existence.

Samuel Woods

Chapter 16: Purpose and Perseverance

The keyword is purpose. How many of us know our purpose in life? T. D. Jakes said, "You need to focus more on your purpose rather than on your problems." That statement is so profound and so true. We tend to focus on whatever goes wrong in our lives rather than on what we can do to make things right. No one is perfect, but we can all work toward perfection as a goal.

When you figure out your purpose, you find your meaning of why you exist. What kind of legacy are you going to leave behind? Finding one's purpose is not easy. It takes a lot of soul-searching. One must know where he or she is going in life. I feel that's why so many of us haven't made anything of our lives. Being stagnated comes from not having proper motivations and aspirations.

Where does one begin? What inspires the passion inside you? Having a passion motivates you, even if you have been dealing with failure your whole life. Who said it was too late to make a change? There is not a soul alive who is perfect. Everyone needs improvement in some area. Whether you want to admit it or not, we all need improvement. Who doesn't want to become better at whatever they're doing? Being established is essential. Accomplishment means that you have reached a goal that you have set.

It is time to think about what's beneficial, not just for yourself but for your family. But you must make sure you are fully prepared to make that transition. You don't want to half-step and play games. Second chances are real, and not many of us get them. So, when you have an opportunity to do something special, you have to take full advantage of that. When you are released from prison, that is a second chance, an opportunity to start over. You get the chance to prove to yourself that you can do better.

Often when we get that second chance, we blow it. We get released and run right back to the same people who were not there for us during the years we just spent in the belly. Despite that, we hang around them and call them our brothers, the same ones who probably helped us land in prison. Why are we loyal to those who are not loyal to us? That was the biggest mistake I ever made in my life, and it took me so many years to figure out that those so-called friends were using me. These were the same guys I grew up with since elementary school, the ones I thought would have my back, stand by me, and help me when I need them. Yet, they turned their backs on me, but I got out and went right back to the hood to be with the same dudes who didn't show any signs of loyalty.

Why do we give loyalty to those who don't reciprocate it? The streets used to honor its rules and codes, but now there is no honor. There was no snitching allowed, and if someone did snitch, he was cut out; the consequences used to be severe. Now nothing happens. The snitches are still allowed to hang around the hood. I mean the rules of the streets have changed dramatically, which made me stop entertaining the thought of living the street life ever again. The game is not being played the same, and everything I have done for my hood was no longer respected. It was like I got spit on. I felt like those I helped, looked out for, and took care of shit on me when I caught a life sentence. When I was in need, those I claimed as my brothers were not there for me. I saw them care more for those who had not done half of what I had for them and everything we stood for. Once I saw how the streets changed, I realized the life I had been living did not hold any weight anymore.

Nobody cares about the laws and rules of the streets because they don't live by the code anymore. Knowing these things did not make my decision easy so much as it made me want to pull away from that life. Once I made that decision with my heart and soul entirely, I was able to stand by everything I have written in this book. Now, it is authentic. It is real. A lot of people want to change but fear what the streets are going to say. The truth is you are not missing anything. If someone who claims to be your friend tries to disown you for wanting to break free from the cycle, they don't care about you. Someone who hands you a gun or a bag of drugs when you fresh out from prison isn't someone who has your best interest at heart. A real friend wouldn't want to see you with another felony on your hands. It doesn't make any sense to me. That's not a real friend, and I'm here to give you a different road to drive on. I've been on both ends. I've received drugs and guns from those so-called friends fresh out, and I've given drugs and weapons to my supposed friends. I was lost and misguided for so many years of my life, not understanding the damage I caused myself and others.

Now I'm looking at myself and where I stand today. I've figured a lot out about myself during this time in prison. One thing I've figured out is that it takes a real man to want to change for the better. Self-awareness is the key. You must know yourself, your weaknesses as well as your strengths. You have to tune in to your inner self. It is hard figuring out who we are. We tend to think we are somebody who we aren't. I think it comes from us wanting to be more than what we are. People pretend all the time. Why? They feel like they need to uphold an image of being something that they are not. We all go through an identity crisis at least has once in our lifetime. I thought I was somebody, but I was selling myself short. Now, my values, morals, and principles would never be compromised for anyone or anything. Standing for something means just that - taking a stand. I will forever stand for the things I believe. I believe anyone can change if they put their hearts into it and say the hell with those old ways. You have to try some new tactics.

I believe we all have something special in us, and we must hold ourselves to a higher standard. What are your expectations? Where do you want to be in two years? In five years? In ten years? You must set short-term goals before you can start doing extraordinary things. Figuring out what is important to you and do what is necessary to reach those goals are the keys to success. Who doesn't want to be successful? Right! We all want to have success in our lives. Yet not everybody has the life they dream of, but how many of us have done everything in our power to be whatever we wanted to be? I'm looking at the reality of everything people are dealing with, how we think, and how we are. You must know your capabilities and understand what you have inside of you to achieve those higher expectations of yourself.

Samuel Woods

Chapter 17: Life Goes On

Most people think you reach the end of your rope when you get incarcerated. But I'm here to tell you that it is not true at all. You may come to an end of living as a free man physically, but freedom is in the mind. Have you ever heard the saying that they can trap my body but can't trap my mind? I may be in prison, but my mind is free, free to gain knowledge and think powerful thoughts. People on the outside don't know that life doesn't stop for those who are locked up. Even people in prison believe everything is on hold until they get released, but that is not true. I have learned that although I'm in prison, I can still express myself and my ideas and create something positive by using my mind. We always think of the worst when we are in bad situations rather than looking at things optimistically and seeing the good that may come of out a bad situation. I never allowed my circumstances to define who I was as a man. Despite the amount of time they gave me, I told myself that I was never going to give up. I remain focused, and I conduct myself with the thoughts that I would soon be released, and the truth would set me free.

I'm looking at how many prisoners take their sentences and just do the time. Others allow the time to do them; they can't take the horrible things that prisons have to offer, and they turn weak. I know many who have hanged themselves. Others have slit their wrists. I have been around a lot of guys who couldn't take the time that was handed down. Being in prison without any support is hard. Some guys can't handle that. Not having family and friends to help financially and emotionally causes incarcerated people to give up; they start doing crazy things because they have been broken down and feel like there is nothing to live for.

I see this all the time still behind these walls because most think about where they are rather than where they can be in the future. Just because you are prison doesn't mean you have to give up. You must continue moving forward. I did. I kept going, and I remained focused on being something better than what I once was. And as I changed my thought process, I began to come up with a lot of ideas toward making positive things happen. Then, I thought about writing a book, not just any kind of book. It needed to have substance, and here we are. I wanted to talk about how we, as convicted felons, are treated without respect or compassion. Not all of us are guilty. Many innocent people are incarcerated. I know many people who have fought to clear their names, but the courts keep denying them on the grounds of them not having their motion filed in a timely fashion. When that happens, the judge time bars you without even looking at the evidence that clears your name. The court system violates our constitutional rights all the time. It gets away with it because most of us are unfamiliar with how the law works and cannot hire competent, honest attorneys to help us. So, we represent ourselves, and they try to find things we didn't do right to deny us rather than looking at the actual merits of our arguments.

Holding someone in prison for 15, 20, or even more years for a crime they did not commit is cruel and unusual punishment at its finest. Yet, what do they get for the wrongdoing of having an innocent person serve more time in prison than they spent living on the streets? It is unfair and unjust. Why isn't any of this being discussed? Why hasn't anything been done to prevent these wrongful convictions? Not long ago, a friend of mine was released after serving 15 years in prison for a murder he did not commit. They had the real culprit in custody admitting it was him, yet my friend sat in prison for years fighting for his freedom. Why did it take 15 years and so many obstacles?

That doesn't make any sense; yet, we are called criminals. What do you call people who sit back and watch an innocent man being mistreated and cheated out of his freedom? He's locked away from his kids and family. He can't get back any of those years they took, yet they try to pacify us with giving us money for the so-called mistake they made. That's what they try to say. They made a mistake, but it was never a mistake; they mean to do everything they do to us. They don't want us to change for the better, and we are so stupid to fall for all the traps they set for us. My mission now is to give us hope and open the eyes of those who may still be walking around blind.

I'm not trying to say that I am better in any way because I am still in the struggle with you. Even if I were to get released tomorrow, I always would be. I want us to start thinking better and start trying to become better than we have been.

Samuel Woods

Chapter 18: Fighting Demons

I know it's hard to change. I'm still working on some flaws. It's natural. No man on earth is perfect, but if you are not trying to improve yourself, then you have already failed. And you should not accept failure. We have been failing for too long. The system has failed us. Our elders have failed us. And our community has failed us. It is time now for us to stand for ourselves and change the pattern. We need to break the cycle of black men falling for the same things that have not gotten us anywhere for generations.

This world needs to change right now more than ever. We have been dealing with so much hate in this world. It seems like every year we have a new struggle. Blacks have been fighting for centuries. It is like no matter how close we get to finally making a difference in the world, more bullshit happens. The list is so long, from the Jena Six Movement to the Trayvon Martin Movement to the riots in Baltimore. In many different situations, we have been fighting for freedom for all of us, not just fighting for the freedom of those who are incarcerated for wrongful imprisonment and cruel and unusual punishment from law enforcement. Even though we have had a black president, we still have not made any progress.

Now there is the "me too" movement, which has been knocking top producers out of their positions and empires. Yet I have not seen any of them on trial. The only one has been Bill Cosby. He did the same thing all these white CEOs have done, lied to an intern about giving them a part in a movie or a promotion to have sex, but he is the only one serving prison time. It is fucked up how being a particular color will determine one's fate, but this is what is happening in this system. We will never be equal, no matter how much we try or how much we accomplish. We had a black president. When that happened, we saw just how these white muthafuckas had fucked this world up. Obama gave us so much hope and so much inspiration. With your aspirations in mind, you must not allow anything stop you from wanting to achieve and conquer.

We must stop using excuses and putting the blame on everyone else. It takes a real man to accept his wrongdoings. Holding yourself accountable for the way you live is a crucial step to take when trying to change. Accountability is powerful within itself, and I hold myself responsible for all the things I did that gotten me taken away from my kids. They gave me a lot of my strength to keep fighting and standing tall, although all the odds have been against me. I stood firm, even when I was standing by myself. I knew I couldn't give up on them. I had to give it my all for my children.

They say God works in mysterious ways, and blessings come when least expected. I'm living full proof of that very statement. I was doing everything in my power to stay on my mission, which was to get a lawyer to help get my freedom back. I had all these people in my life who I knew could have easily given up the money to get me a lawyer, yet they chose not to. My so-called friends who I knew had thousands of dollars told me they didn't have it. They didn't even stop by and check on my mother when she had two heart attacks and a stroke. I saw the fake love of my so-called friends.

I used to say, "Aye, Bro, I need whatever you can do for me to help with this lawyer." My cries for help fell on deaf ears. Even my brother basically told me to go to hell. He said I was never getting out, and I was going to do the entire 30 years they gave me. I was so hurt; I could not believe I heard these words from someone I had looked up to my whole life, someone I had respected. I couldn't believe he was treating me like this and saying some of the things he was saying. What made it worse was our mother was on the phone, so she heard every word, but she didn't say anything. I tried to explain to him the things I had and was trying to do, but he wasn't trying to hear it. He said he refused to give another dollar to pay a lawyer who he knew couldn't get me out. He felt like since they gave me a life sentence, I was guilty, and it was over for me. He studied the law for one year and thought he knew what he was talking about. He didn't account for all the positive things I had going for me. We didn't speak for years after that phone call.

Imprisonment

It felt like my brother was against me. I felt so alone. I didn't have anybody. I had thought I was all that on the streets. All the laws and rules of the streets went out the window. I hadn't received any loyalty from any of my guys from the same hood I did so much for, yet I didn't allow it to get me down. I just kept it solid within myself and stayed focused. I was on a mission.

Samuel Woods

Chapter 19: Green-Eyed Blessings

After I got dropped down from a level four to a three, I landed in Mansfield Correctional Institution. I was eager to begin my mission and start my journey toward my freedom. I had a couple of female friends I used to talk to when I was home, and another I met once I got to Mansfield that was there for me. They helped me take care of some things, and I appreciated all the love they showed, but it just wasn't enough. They showed me love and gave me a lot of support, but something was missing. They couldn't provide what I needed, and at that time, I didn't know what it was. But after being in Mansfield for one month, I embraced so many blessings. They came in a flurry, and I just grabbed hold of them, and I took full advantage of every one of them.

I was able to obtain some money, and then I made a powerful connection with a woman who remembered me from years before. We started to build and talk and get to know one another. She was beautiful, smart, and had so many things going on when I first met her. I had some things going on as well, but I was so intrigued by her. Right off the bat, I could see how compatible we were; we connected on so many levels. Everything just felt right to me. After months of us talking and building on our friendship, she still never asked me why I was doing 35 to life in prison. That is one of the reasons I knew she was different. As we became closer, I saw that she was what I needed in my life. She felt the same way about me.

What was so crazy was I was trying to talk to so many girls at one time that I accidentally called her by another woman's name, not even realizing I just had fucked up. She forgave me and continued to talk to me. That's when I knew she was meant for me. It was fate. Any other girl would have felt disrespected and left me alone. That's just the thing. People will leave you when it is an easy option as opposed to taking a chance and fighting for something that could be special. When I called her another female's name, we had not even made a connection or anything yet. She didn't have any reason to keep wanting to talk to me, yet she did. We started building something powerful that has brought so much positivity into my life.

After five months of building and getting to know each other, really digging deep into one another's pasts and just figuring out what the other really was about, I told her my situation. I told her how I was in prison for murder. I was innocent, and I was fighting to get my freedom back. She didn't take off running. She didn't judge. She didn't say, "Well, I'm sorry. You're doing too much time for a crime I strongly disagree with." She didn't do any of that. Instead, she said, "What do we have to do to make this right?" I was so surprised and at a loss for words. I was blown away by her reaction. I knew right then and there that she was real, and she really loved me. All the other females who had been in my life decided they could not do the time or felt I was holding them back. They thought I was never getting out of prison. All these females I had known for years turned their backs on me rather than having my back.

Suddenly, I had a beautiful, strong woman asking what we needed to do to make this situation right. I was convinced that she was brought to me by God, and I was going to cherish her for as long as I lived. After she showed me that she was willing to fight with and for me, there was nothing else left for me to do but lock it in and make her my woman. I think she had that in her plans all along because before I could even tell her I wanted her to be my woman, she already was telling me to cut all my "hoes off" in her words. She was serious. At the time, I was in the hole for being caught up in a gang fight. Instead of pulling away, she drew closer. She came and saw me behind a glass window. For our first visit, we were separated by a glass window. We couldn't touch. We couldn't kiss each other for the first time. It was a sad moment for both of us, and she just broke down in tears. I sat behind that glass window looking into the pretty green eyes of this beautiful woman who had given up so much to be with me and saw the pain inside her because her man was locked up. That shit had me going through it. That's when I decided to cut all those hoes off. She was all I needed.

Imprisonment

I did just that, although it was hard to cut a couple of them off. I had one that was there for me since I first came to prison, but she wasn't fighting for my freedom. She didn't care if I did it or not. She just was there for me. That is what I had been missing. She fought for me, but the other one didn't care about my freedom like she did. That's when I knew she was the one. A couple of months after I was let out of the hole, I asked her to marry me. Of course, she said yes. I never thought I would ask anyone to marry me. It was crazy, but it felt so right, and I never had real love like this in my life before. She brings so many good things in my life. Yes, I am serving a life sentence, but we didn't allow that to dictate our lives and take anything away from our love and our mission to get the truth heard in my case.

She is everything I needed to move forward on this new journey. I give my wife so much credit for the transition I've made. She made me want to be better in every way. She has challenged me in every way possible. She is the reason I am turning my life around. I say that because I saw her turn her life around and really make something of it. In one year, we both have changed drastically. You know how they say when you find the one for you, everything in your life will change? I swear it went just like that. The more I did good things and worked toward positive things, the more blessings started to come for my wife and me. We were able to retain a lawyer and get the information we needed for the truth to come out about my case. Now, we are remaining focused on getting my freedom back.

It has been a rough road I have been driving on, and it feels like, at any given moment, the tires are going to blow. But the powerful love from my wife gives me the strength to make it to the next day. When I feel weak and defeated, she reminds me that I am strong and about what we have together. It took everything we had in us to obtain it, so we must stay on track and finish this journey on a strong note. Even now, the feeling is so refreshing. It feels good to be married to the most incredible women in the world.

We had so many challenges dealing with getting married inside a prison. Friends and family couldn't believe she was about to marry someone who was not only serving a life sentence but for murder. It was hard for her to try to prove to her family that I am not only innocent but that I am with her for all the right reasons. They thought I was trying to use her and just could not believe that we could be genuinely in love. I know it sounds crazy, but you can't limit love, and you can't dictate when you find your soulmate. People are placed in your life for different reasons, and you just don't know why until it happens to you. Love is love. Love is powerful, and anyone who believes in love knows that. You can't fight real love when you find it. It will overpower all things.

Even after we married, my family couldn't believe it. They didn't understand why a woman would want to marry a man who is serving such a long sentence. My mother was the only person who showed even a little support, so we are in this by ourselves. That is how it has been – just the two of us.

After not receiving any support from our families, we faced another challenge. We had been approved to be married; the lawyer came, and I signed my marriage papers. The only thing left was for us to have our ceremony. The warden had to sign off on the visit for us to have the wedding ceremony. He denied the visit, saying our marriage was a threat to the institution, and we were trying to bring drugs into his prison. None of this made any sense. My wife had been coming to see me every week and never had any issues. It felt like he wanted to take away our happiness, although he does not have the power to do that. The warden's little stunt didn't stop my wife. She is relentless. She made sure we had our ceremony; we just had to improvise.

We were wed on December 11, 2017, the best and most amazing day of my life. I know you are probably wondering how that could be since I am still in prison. That's the thing. Although I was incarcerated, I was still living my life. I didn't give the doubters the satisfaction of me being miserable or me giving up in any kind of way. I continued to live my life as if I was not locked up. I made sure to let them see that no matter what they tried to do, they couldn't break me, and of course, they hated it. They want to see us beat down and broken, miserable with no hope. But it is essential for us not to allow that to happen despite the difficulties we face in prison.

Finding my wife gave new meaning to my life. I had someone else to live for. She has brought so much positivity into my life. She has made me look at things differently; her lack of judgment against me inspires me to be a better man. That is how I knew her love was real. She looked past the exterior circumstances and saw me. She read my case and saw that I was innocent and started to fight even harder for me. She already believed me when I told her

I was innocent, but after she read the evidence, she saw that the system is a big joke.

Love is powerful. Love can help get you through so many things in your life, especially pain and hardship. My wife has given me so much love that it helped get me through the hardest of the hardest time in my life. I really began to open my mind and let my heart follow, to become more than just a prison inmate. I needed to reach deep inside my soul and work on all the things that were holding me back from making progress toward a righteous life. My motto is *Elevate, Execute, and Expand*. That involves taking charge of the way you want your life to be. We can't keep letting the system — the cops, the judges, and the prosecutors win. We must start using our brains. We are smart, strong, and dynamic. If we stand up for ourselves, we can start making a change, which would lead to lower crime rates and less recidivism.

Samuel Woods

Chapter 20: Elevate, Execute, and Expand

My whole purpose for writing this book is to give us hope. I'm talking about the black man who has 2/3/4 prison numbers *and* the ones who are on their way to catching their first felonies. I want to reach those who need to make significant life changes to help and guide them in the right direction. I want to bring awareness to criminal system realities and the way minorities are treated. I want to provide inspiration to those who never felt inspired. I want my story to be a learning experience for those who didn't have guidance nor direction.

Elevate your mind, and then you can take your life to the next level. Once you figure out everything and the route you want to take, you must execute the plan and complete your mission. It is time for us to stop using excuses, pointing fingers, and blaming everybody but ourselves. We have to accept responsibility for the wrong decisions we have made in our life. When you take full responsibility for your actions, you can find a way to move forward. Most of us have a problem with that or just refuse to accept responsibility. That is what you must do as a man: take responsibility and take charge of your life.

It is quite simple, but we make it difficult. I don't know why we do, but I do know we need to start valuing and loving ourselves. Self-love is powerful because then you can give love. You must release that hate you have bottled up inside of you so you can love. I had so much anger and hatred built up inside that it hampered my growth. I couldn't grow because I was still holding hard feelings toward those who claimed they loved me but were not there for me when I needed them the most. That hatred only stopped me from being able to grow and spread my wings and rise to my highest potential. I think that is where most of us fall short. We can be so full of anger and hatred toward someone or something in our lives that we cannot move forward. We can't adjust, and it leaves us vulnerable. Being vulnerable means being transparent. And transparency is something we are not good with because we all try to put on a front. We try to keep that image alive. Instead of working on the problems, we live in denial, which leads to self-destruction.

Depression is a serious issue both inside and outside of these prison cells. I think we all have dealt with depression at some point in our lives. Depression can lead us to not thinking clearly. It can cloud our judgment and negatively impact our decision-making. I used to get depressed and become violent. The prison system is not equipped to manage the severity of depression inmates face. I believe it has a lot to do with one's behavior. Sadness and anger are signs of depression, and if you are feeling any of those things, you need to talk with someone. You must work on your emotions and anger. I believe the best way to manage your emotions is to focus your energy on something you like to do, like reading a book, playing sports, or exercising. Find an activity to help you keep your mind off the things that make you feel angry and sad.

I received a lot of support from my aunt Sharon, who is a minister, while I was in the hole at Lucasville. I was at a point in my life where I needed to change my way of thinking and really work on my anger, so I really started to read in the Bible and take it seriously. With my aunt's help, I expanded my thought processes and did a lot of soul-searching. I worked on clearing all those bad habits and evil thoughts out of my mind. She started sending her Wednesday service Bible studies as well as studies from Reverend Charles Stanley, which helped me a lot. I also was attending a Bible class with a group from Cross Road Bible Institute. I graduated and earned a diploma upon completing my courses. I learned so much when I took on that challenge. I didn't expect to gain so much knowledge and strength as well as awareness of who I am. I thought I knew myself, but I didn't. During that year, I spent in the hole, I made the changes that were needed to handle different situations better than I did before, and I really loved that. I love how much I grew in that year. It was very fulfilling, and I now understand where a lot of my problems came from. Once you figure out the issues you have with yourself, you can start figuring out how to solve them.

Imprisonment

Let me say this. Nothing happens overnight. You must work at it and work at it and work at it. Even after that year, I really dug into my inner self. I still had an anger problem, but I learned how to control my temper. Now, whenever I get mad, I think things through. In the past, I would just react and not think about the consequences of my actions, which usually ended badly. Doing things off impulse typically does not end well. But as I grew and worked on my anger, I found a way I could balance it to the point it didn't put me in compromising positions. We must find an outlet through something that can help us focus and keep our minds on the right things. We need to learn how to love ourselves better, which will lead to living a better life.

There is something else we all must learn while you have the chance to. We all must learn patience. Patience is essential. If most of us had patience, then most of us wouldn't be incarcerated. And that's a fact. They say being incarcerated helps you become patient. Yes, that is true because you are at a standstill. Sitting in one place for an extended period teaches patience. Still, it is what you do with that patience is what matters most. I did ten years straight. You would have thought I would have learned patience while I was incarcerated. Yet, when I came home, I was moving so fast I didn't even realize how out of balance I was. I was heading nowhere fast. I wasn't thinking. I was just moving without knowing where I was headed. That's just it. While we are out in the streets, we are just living day-to-day. We should know where we are going and what we are living for in life. Once you find whatever it is you think you are supposed to be doing, you need to put everything you have into everything you need to do to conquer that something. Once we find out or purpose and what our calling is, that helps guide how we live the rest of our lives.

Purpose helps with changing our behavior patterns. I really want to see us changing our lives. I want to see every released felon get out, follow all the requirements, do the things they are supposed to, and accomplish meaningful goals. On top of staying focused, we must stop with the genocide. I used to be at war with my own kind. It took many years to realize all that hatred toward my own was not helping anybody except the oppressor. Killing one another, whether with a gun, knife, or drugs, is genocide. Our community needs to talk about it and develop strategies to end it. Gang banging has gotten so weak. Ask yourself why we are at war. What do we get out of going to war with each other? It seems like we would rather fight each other than fight to change the legal system and the ones who give your brother 15 years for robbing a store or your uncle five years for having a gun in his possession. Why don't we ever come together and do things that are right for us as a community? The laws leave us trapped in a system that violates our constitution rights daily, but I don't see anybody walking to the courthouse and taking a stand against the shady justice system. Yet, we go against each other. We can make a difference if we take a stand together and fight for our rights instead of killing each other over nothing.

I used to think I was fighting for a cause when I was going to war with other hoods. I did not even realize I was doing the oppressors a favor and giving the cops what they want. They want to see us fighting each other. They want to see us killing one another off as opposed to working together to make something of our communities. After years of growth, you come to understand that there is a better life to live. You start to see that all you were doing does not add up to anything but prison time and loss of some of your best friends to the violence. The quicker we realize all that shooting each other adds up to nothing, the faster we can create change.

We know what we must do, but we miss opportunities that present themselves. That is a big issue. I think we lack confidence. We deserve to be successful and to accomplish our goals. We are unique and have gifts that others wish they had. I have seen some of the most talented people in prison. I have come across guys who played basketball so well that I would wonder why they were in prison instead of in the NBA. I have met fantastic football players who leave you at a loss for words when you think about all the talent they possess that was once taken for granted. There are rappers and singers in prison who are more talented than the people you hear on the radio, but they took the wrong route, and the streets took away their future. When I see that, I get frustrated because it is so hard to make it out of the hood, and a few wrong decisions stripped these guys of better opportunities. Some of them may have made the wrong decision because they did not have anyone in their lives to help them stay focused and on the right track. Our kids lose when we don't give them the encouragement they need to keep them on the road to success.

Chapter 21: Guiding Generations

We need to focus on the youth and our children and ensure they feel our love and support. We must be there for our kids. We must pay attention to them and learn what it is they like and want to accomplish in life. Although my mother used to try to keep me focused, I just was too much for her to handle. She could not stop me from doing what I wanted to do, which led to me getting into trouble. You must be a constant presence in your kid's lives early on and help mold them into wonderful citizens. Teach them the importance of values, morals, principles, and respect for themselves and others. We must keep the kids away from the streets and do not allow them to have friends that are negative influences.

Most of the time, when kids start getting into trouble, it is because of the company they are keeping, so make sure they are around positive people. If you are around nine positive people every day, you will most likely become the tenth. Spending time with your kids helps them and you. I have seen many guys get released and spend more time running the streets chasing females and wanting to kick it in clubs with their friends rather than spending time with their kids. That is a big problem. There is nothing more important than family, especially the kids. You must give your kids the love and affection they need and deserve. Nothing should ever come before your kids. If we all looked at life that way, we would do better by our kids and our families because when you go to prison, the kids are the ones that suffer the most.

Knowing I allowed myself to be taken away from my kids because of a life sentence really fucked with me mentally. It has caused me to reevaluate everything and everyone in my life to the point I have done away with everything and everyone who means me no good. Since I have done that, I have felt better about myself, and good things have been happening for me. I have learned to cherish my kids and to never take them for granted ever again.

We all have taken some of the most precious things in life for granted in our lives. Hopefully, we have recognized and made up for it. That is hard to do from prison. Time is precious, and you must use it wisely. You have to take everything seriously every day. That is not to say you can't laugh and joke and enjoy your life, but you must put yourself in a good situation for your kids and you. Being the biggest supporter of your family means everything. Life is not easy. We must work hard for what we want.

Coming from a prison cell, you must work even harder, but if you work hard, you will make it through the obstacles life throws at you. You just must prepare yourself for everything to come and focus on what you are trying to accomplish. Do not allow anyone to tell you that you can't achieve what you want to; just remain keyed in on your goals. When life gets hard, pray, and stay positive. There is power in prayer. You don't have to believe in Jesus Christ. Just understanding that there is a higher power than you is enough. My mother calls the prayer line to make prayer requests for me to this day, and I know that positive energy is surfacing when good things happen. Find something you believe in and keep your spiritual life alive.

You will be surprised by what kind of doors open for you when you believe and have faith. Belief is powerful. Believe in yourself. Believe that you can and you will make it through anything. If you can make it through prison sane and stronger than what you were when you first went in, then you can make it on the streets. Prison is no different from the streets. The same rules apply; the only difference is the location. You have to be ready to do everything in your power to become better than that number they gave you. Stop selling yourself short. I know you are tired of going through the same thing, so try to do right. It is so easy to do all the wrong things. We continue to repeat the pattern that is killing us. I have become so fed up with the same results, the repeated prison time being served. If you are fed up too, use that as motivation to change your life.

We are so much smarter than what they try to make of us. We have so much to offer besides what we have been demonstrating. We all have a job to do as individuals, and that is to change the cycle. The problem starts with us having kids and then leaving our kids' mothers to fend for themselves. This is where the problem begins. We need to change the way we treat the women in our lives. Raising children alone is hard. Raising sons alone can be even harder because a woman does not always know how to teach a boy to become a man. Many of us used to run all over our mothers; that's probably why we were running the streets. We didn't have a man in our lives to give us direction and teach us another way to live.

That is why you have to be there physically and emotionally to show your kids the right path. It starts with us. The man is the head of every family. We must raise boys and girls to be honorable men and women. How can we do that if we are in a prison cell? It is hard, and our kids deserve better. They need their fathers. If you don't want your kids following you in your footsteps, you have to set a better example. We must give our children the tools they need to become something in life. You always want your kids to be better than you, but if you are not feeding them positive things, then they will go down the same path you did. I have seen many fathers in prison with their son's standing right next to them. That is a sad sight. Who wants to have their son standing in prison with them? I have never heard a father say he wanted his kids to follow him into prison, but if you are not setting a good example, what can you expect? If you are not a positive role model, how do you expect them to do righteous things?

You must lead by example. Kids want to follow in their parent's footsteps. If you are showing them a life of crime, what type of lives do you think they will live? We have to change our ways and guide the children onto a more productive path.

I have many regrets, but everything that has happened to me has brought me to this point of writing a book that sheds light on the way the court system is being run and how we break the cycle. I have gained this knowledge and want to share it to help guide those that are trying to change their lives. I know you are tired of being stuck in the cycle of getting locked up repeatedly, so what are you going to do about it? We all want to make that transition; we just don't know how or where to start.

Samuel Woods

Chapter 22: Activist Spirit

You have to start at the heart of it all right in the hoods. But who is willing to take on that fight? I have a solution for my city that I feel it will help. I'm taking on the role of being a gang activist. I will be fighting for the transitions of gang members. My job will be showing these young guys that being in a gang is not the only route they have to take. It is going to be my duty to show them another way, to help them envision more than what they see in front of them. There is more to life than selling drugs and banging blocks and hoods. Still, it is up to us to show them that they can be somebody even though they think they don't have what it takes to be anything other than a drug dealer or gang member. We tend to think we can't be or do something just because we have not tried or had the means to make it happen, but that is just us thinking small and not having any faith in ourselves.

It is my mission to motivate those who need to make a change in their life. I want to start with the juveniles, so I can reach them while their still young to help change their direction before they become statistics, although it is never too late to change or learn. Growth has no limitations. You see 40-year-olds attending college because growing and gaining knowledge is essential. There is no time capsule on gaining an education. I want to grab the minds and hearts of the young before they get into the system.

I feel my *Cure Gang Violence Movement* will do just that. That is not to say I will not fight for those who are already in the system. They will receive proper care, as well. I want us to use our minds more positively. We have some of the most intelligent minds, yet we seem to use our brains in the wrong manner. We take our incredible visions and use them to commit crimes and try to be a smarter criminal. I used to think that when I got caught for something, I would see where I went wrong so I can do it better next time. That is stupid, because why would you want to do something again that you already went to jail for? This is why you see people with numerous drug charges on their record. You have to think to yourself that if you keep getting caught for the same thing, then you are not good at it. Maybe you should try to do something different and positive. When is enough going to really be enough?

We need a program for those who are fresh out of prison to provide all the resources one needs such as, shelter, food, and a job. If most of us had these things when we were released from prison, it would relieve the pressure of getting money illegally so we can eat and sleep.

We are hung up on the thought that money is everything. Okay, you need money, but money is not everything. That is where we go wrong. Thinking money is everything leads us to do anything for it, even if it means risking our freedom. This is not the way to go about getting money, and it is not even the money that people are chasing. It is the things they want to buy, the material things. I know a lot of people who buy things they want rather than the things they need. We have been brainwashed to seek materialistic things rather than making an honest living and using the money to take care of our families. Our kids are being influenced by videos. The rapper is draped with the chains, gold rings, designer clothes, pretty women, and rapping a verse about how they got the money and jewelry from selling drugs. So, all kids want these days is to be a rapper, to have money and gold chains. We must teach our kids another path to take to get money.

Everybody thinks you have to hustle drugs to be a hustler. That is not true. You can have two jobs and be that same hustler. Hustling doesn't mean you have to sell drugs or do anything illegal. You can be a hustler working a good job. If you are making money, you are a hustler. Many have come to believe that we have to be doing something illegal to make money, but that is not necessary. You just do not realize that because you have not been shown any other way, and you have a one-track mind. You don't know, but I'm here to give you the real. Let me tell you about this money that has so many of us lost. Money is the root of all evil because a person would do anything to obtain it. Money can drive people to steal from their own families. Money can cause people to rise up against their brothers, best friends, even their own mothers. Some people would kill family members for money. Money is the reason the world is so fucked up right now and why there isn't any honor or loyalty. I have seen many people sell their souls for money and give up all their values and principles for some money, but money comes and goes. Just as fast as you get the cash, you lose it. Look at how many movie stars or musicians have gone from having millions of dollars to being dead broke.

We need to change the minds of those who think money is everything to the point they would break laws to obtain it. We have to teach our children the value of a dollar and to righteously knowing within that money is earned by working hard for it. It will last longer, and they will respect it more. Those who don't respect money are broke or keep going to prison trying to get it.

Getting money isn't hard; keeping money is the hard part because when some people finally do get some money, they don't know what to do with it. They spend it on meaningless things. They want to look fly yet have not paid their bills and owe back child support. They just don't want to take care of their business, and I hate that we are like that. I was wasting my life trying to do things I had no business doing for the mighty dollar. Yet, the money didn't solve any problems. Everybody thinks once they get some money, it will solve all their problems, but it won't. It may help with some issues, but not solve them. Money will never solve your problems when you are dealing with your internal issues. Dealing with your inner self requires more than money. This problem is more profound than the dollar. Once we realize the real richness is within our minds and hearts, we will accomplish more. We all are rich, but we are broken. Coming from broken homes, we have to be rebuilt so we can live abundant lives, rich in soul, mind, body, and heart. Anybody can make money if they put their minds to doing something productive for the money. When we realize cash will not solve all our problems, fewer people will try to commit crimes to obtain it.

The time has come for us to really start using our brains and stop playing. We have to start somewhere, and I am willing to do whatever it takes I can to get this message across. But I cannot do it alone. I need you to make that transition and really see and understand that there is more in life for you than being another prison number or murder statistic. We have to start taking life seriously now and make the necessary adjustments. You know what you have to do. Fuck all that pride you have bottled up inside you. Let that pride out and spread your wings to the highest heights. You have to have integrity no matter what life has already thrown at you. Someone else has been through more than you have, so it is not about that. We are not keeping track of who has been through more than the next. We are more concerned about who wants to break through and make something of themselves, find their true selves, become something, and be somebody to their kids and family instead of being the same big old mistake. Fuck that! We are not making excuses anymore. We are making power moves toward greatness.

I know you have it in you. I was one of the hardest of the hard, yet I made the decision to change, not just for myself or my kids and family, but for you. I made the change so I could show you that you can too. We all have it in us to change. I know a lot of us are tired of living the way we have been. We just don't know what to do. I am here to tell you that you will figure it out. Just follow your heart. Your heart and mind are powerful. You can and will do whatever you put your mind to if you put your heart into it. Watch, you will see. If you are incarcerated right now, please dig deep inside yourself, find what it is you want out of life. Then fight for that. Be that person that can make a change and make a difference. And if you are on the streets, I want you to find it in your heart to give yourself a chance to become something great without having to go through being imprisoned before you make a change. Be great now. Be smart. Be someone that can look back and say they turned their lives around before they destroyed them. You will be so proud of yourself for doing the smartest thing you probably could have done in your life. Break the cycle.

Life is what you make it. What kind of life do you want to make for yourself?

"Injustice anywhere is a threat to justice everywhere."
– Martin Luther King, Jr.

About the Author

Samuel Woods currently is incarcerated in North Central Correctional Institution serving a 35-years to life sentence for murder. He has been in prison for 6 ½ years.

Mr. Woods has a beautiful and loving wife, Ashley Woods, and two wonderful children, Samuel Woods, Jr. and Daeshona Miller, who both are 17 years old.

Mr. Woods is fighting for justice in his case and wants those who are in a similar situation to continue to fight. Never give up. Mr. Woods encourages you to go to your legal library and learn everything you can learn about the law. They hide the truth from us, and if you don't read and search for the information, you will never know what rights they may be violating. Continue to fight for justice and liberty.

If you have any questions for Mr. Woods, you can contact him at:

Samuel Woods #643-356
NCCC
PO Box 1812
Marion, Ohio 43302
https://booksbytheshelf.org

www.ingramcontent.com/pod-product-compliance
Lightning Source LLC
Chambersburg PA
CBHW071501080526
44587CB00014B/2173